CHOICES:

A Teen Woman's Journal for Self-awareness and Personal Planning

Written by Mindy Bingham, Judy Edmondson
and Sandy Stryker
Edited by Dennis Coon, Sevren Coon and
Barbara Greene
Designed by Margaret Dodd
Illustrated by Rose Margaret Braiden,
Pam Hoeft and Itoko Maeno

Advocacy Press, Santa Barbara, California

For Lucile Graham and Eleanor Van Cott

Copies of this book may be ordered by sending
$16.45 ppd. to <u>Choices</u>, Advocacy Press, P.O. Box 236,
Santa Barbara, CA 93102. (California residents add
sales tax.)

Proceeds from the sale of this book will benefit the
Girls Club of Santa Barbara, Inc., and contribute to the
further development of programs for girls and young
women aged 6 to 18.

Copyright © 1984 by Girls Club of Santa Barbara, Inc.,
Updated 1987
531 East Ortega Street, Santa Barbara, California 93103,
an affiliate of Girls Clubs of America, Inc.
Library of Congress Card No. 82-074535
ISBN 0-911655-22-0

 Published by Advocacy Press, P.O. Box 236,
Santa Barbara, California 93102

Printed in the United States of America

12 11 10

This book belongs to _Sharon Tal-Garodnick_

Age _13_

I began my entries on _Aug 2, 1989_

I finished my entries on _____

My workbook is dedicated to _My future,_
hoping it'll be a good
one. And to my parents who
try to make it the best.

Include snapshots of yourself here.

Sail on, silver girl,
Sail on by.
Your time has come to shine.
All your dreams are on their way.
— Paul Simon
    "Bridge Over Troubled
    Water"

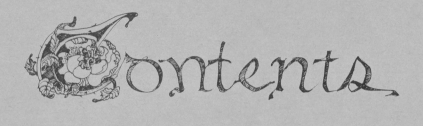
Contents

"Where do I go from here?" asked Mary Catherine Pomfretz. She knew what she had — three pair of running shoes, a B plus average in school, the best record collection in her class, and a problem complexion. To some extent, she also knew what she wanted — clear skin and a date with Matt Roberts.

Yet, thinking about the future — especially the future beyond next Saturday night — was a new experience for Mary Catherine. It was exciting to imagine the adventures that might await her, but it was worrisome, too. Would she go to college? Would she be able to find a job? Would she get married? Would she have children? How would she know what was right for _her_?

Mary Catherine, like all young women today, had to make some difficult decisions. Wisely, she realized that it was not too soon to begin thinking about them. It's time for you to begin thinking about your future, too. This book is designed to help you do that.

You may not have realized it yet, but this book is about you: your dreams, your thoughts, and your plans. To make it yours, you will need to be an active participant. We have included some exercises which have been helpful to other young women. To make the most of your journey through this book, you should complete them as you read. There are also pages at the end of each section in which you are asked to record your own thoughts about the ideas just covered.

If you turn to the back of the book, you'll find pages that are not to be completed until you're older. They're there because, as long as you live, you will continue to grow and change. You'll have new opportunities, and new decisions to make. When the time comes, this section will help you make better decisions in your life.

We think you'll find this is a book you'll want to keep. Someday you may want to pass it on to your daughter or to another special young woman in your life. The final product will be the story of your life as planned, directed, and written by you. What could be more special than that?

I want to be all that I am capable of
becoming. . . .
— Katherine Mansfield
Journal, 1922

Introduction

It's hard to be a team player when
they don't want you on their team.
— Rosabeth Moss Kanter

A long habit of not thinking a thing
<u>wrong</u> gives it the superficial
appearance of being <u>right</u>.
— Thomas Paine
<u>Common Sense</u>

CHAPTER ONE

Not Such Great Expectations

Attitudes and where they come from

9

As a little girl, did you ever wonder what became of Snow White, Cinderella, and Sleeping Beauty after they married their princes and retired to their respective castles? It's possible that they spent the rest of their lives happily playing bridge, experimenting with make-up, and redecorating the throne room. Yet, maybe one of them was forced to support the family when an unexpected revolution in the kingdom left her prince jobless. (Former princes are highly unemployable.) Maybe one of them was banished for being so fond of the castle pastry that she outgrew her royal cape. Or, perhaps, one grew so bored with the castle routine that she decided she needed to do something for herself.

If these things happened — and they might have — what kind of jobs could they get? Like most women, they were brought up to believe that if they were cute and charming, someday their prince would appear. He would take care of them, provide for them, and worry about the future. In return, they would give up their independence and the ability to support themselves.

Today we know that being unable to support yourself is a risky way to live. Here's the bad news: About half of all marriages end in divorce. More married women now must work just to help pay the bills. Women outlive men by an average of about eight years. Of course, many women are choosing to skip marriage altogether in order to devote more time to their careers or other activities; but that's not necessarily bad news. The point, simply put, is that women need to be able to make enough money to support themselves.

Here's the good news: There are thousands of ways for you to do that. Your generation of young women has more options for earning a livelihood than previous ones. While only a few years ago most women who worked outside the home were found in only a few job categories — teaching, nursing, clerical work, or retail sales — it is now acceptable for a woman to be anything from an astronaut to a zoo keeper. Your imagination and ambition are the only limitations.

Look around you. Many women are combining careers with marriage and children. Others have decided not to marry at all. There are single-parent families, childless marriages, and families in which the woman has an outside job, while the man takes major responsibility for child care and housework. Which choices appeal to you most?

This book is devoted to helping you make the best decisions for *you*. The time to start thinking about your future is *now*.

Your Life — Present and Future Visions

What is your life like right now? How do you expect it to change as you grow older? The following exercise asks you to consider three important parts of your life — your living conditions, your primary activity, and the most significant people in your life — now and in the future.

Your living conditions refer to both your town and the kind of housing you have or want (apartment, home of your own, etc.). Would you like to live in another part of the country? Do you want to purchase a home by the time you're 30?

Your primary activity refers to the way you spend most of your day. Right now, going to school is probably your primary activity. Perhaps you have a part-time job as well. In a moment you're going to look ahead to view yourself at future ages. When you do, be as specific as possible about what you might be doing. Could it be: Taking care of small children? Working as a mechanic and raising a family? Working as a musician? What would you find most rewarding?

The people closest to you need not be named. They might include parents, husband, children or friends.

A chart for Cinderella showing her living conditions, activities and close relationships at various ages might look something like what you see here. After you read hers, try making one of your own.

CINDERELLA'S LIFE

Age	Where She Lives	Jobs or Major Activities	People Closest to Her
15	Humble cottage with many fireplaces	Taking orders Cleaning fireplaces Manicuring fingernails	Stepmother Stepsisters
20	Same as above	Growing pumpkins Raising white mice Taking charm course by correspondence Learning to walk in glass slippers without screaming in pain	Fairy Godmother
30	Castle	Raising young prince Trying to remain the way she was when the prince fell in love with her Soaking feet	Husband Son Therapist
40	Kingdom University	Taking art and design courses Starting consciousness-raising group Spending weekends with son	Son Friends
60	Co-op apt. in big city	Designing attractive and comfortable shoes for women Spending time with granddaughter, who will be the first princess to rule the kingdom	Friends Son Daughter-in-law Granddaughter

Now, make up a chart for yourself.

ENVISION YOUR LIFE

Age	Where You Live	Jobs or Major Activities	People Closest to You
Present	Capa Cool Mass white ranch house	School	Parents + brother Richard
20	My own little apartment	I head am going to the University	My boyfriend + other friends and still My brother + parents
30	I live in a beautiful house over looking the water	I am now a famous Journalist	My husband + My kids + My brother + parents
40	I live now in a bigger nicer house still on the water	I am now the editor of a famous Magazine	My husband, kids + brother
60	I live in the same house for the winter and have another summer home	I now own this famous magazine but still work as the editor	My husband, kids, brother, & friends, & Grandkids

You've just speculated about your future. Let's explore a little more. Keep your mind open. The sky's the limit!

Attitudes: Will Yours Limit Your Opportunities or Insure Your Success?

Your life choices are affected by attitudes — your own, and the world's. Because these attitudes play such an important part in your life, we must examine them carefully. Women today, as we have already noted, have more freedom and choices than ever before. Sometimes it can be confusing.

Since the changing role of women will affect your future, it's important to know how you feel now. Your opinions will create your attitude toward womanhood and work. Ultimately they will determine how you fit into the picture. To help sort out your opinions, complete the following exercise.

ATTITUDE INVENTORY[1]

Instructions: Put a check mark in the column that best describes how you feel.

	Strongly Agree	Agree	Undecided	Disagree	Strongly Disagree
1. Women with preschool children should not work outside the home.					✓
2. The mother should be awarded custody of the children when a couple is divorced.			✓		
3. Divorced men should not have to assume support for their children.					✓
4. Boys are more intelligent than girls.					✓✓
5. If a working couple buys a house, the husband should make the house payments.					✓
6. At work, women are entitled to use sick leave for maternity leave.			✓		
7. If a woman works outside the home, she should be responsible for the housework as well.					✓

	Strongly Agree	Agree	Undecided	Disagree	Strongly Disagree
8. I would vote for a woman for president if she were the best candidate.	✓				
9. Women are less responsible than men.					✓
10. It is important for a man to be "masculine" and a woman to be "feminine."		✓			✗
11. Men should not cry.					✓
12. Money spent on athletics should be evenly divided between boys and girls.	✓				
13. Both men and women can be good doctors.	✓				
14. Wives should make less money at their jobs than their husbands.					✓
15. Boys should have more education than girls.					✓
16. Women should not hold jobs on the night shift.					✓
17. Men should not do clerical work because they lack the necessary hand dexterity.					✓
18. Women are capable administrators.	✓				⊘ mistake
19. Women should concentrate on finding jobs in the fields of nursing, teaching, clerical and secretarial work since they already possess these skills.					✓
20. A wife and husband should take turns staying home with a sick child.	✓				
21. A single man is not capable of taking care of an infant.	✓		✗		

As you look back over your answers, take a moment to think about why you feel the way you do. Talk to your friends about your thoughts. Then think about your answers again.

By constantly examining your feelings, you continue to grow and learn.

Attitudes and Opinions: Where Do They Come From?

Your family, friends, society's expectations, your observations, TV, radio, newspapers and more, all have helped develop your opinions. We will examine some of these opinion-makers on the next pages.

Your Family

A four-year-old boy whose mother is a lawyer and whose father is a teacher announced, "I'm going to be a teacher when I grow up." "Why not a lawyer?" he was asked. "Only mommies are lawyers," he said.

What you see and hear within your own family will greatly influence *your* thoughts and feelings. Even if you disagree with your family, you may subconsciously adopt many of its attitudes.

What have you learned from your family? Do you want your future family to share these beliefs? The following exercise will help you decide.

Who is currently a member of your family (mother, father, step-parent, brother, sister, etc.)?

Mother, Father & brother

When you are an adult, whom will you include in your ideal family? For example, husband and two children? Husband but no children? Parents? Yourself only?

Husband and two children

What messages or information do you receive from your family?

This may take a little detective work. Unless you're very lucky, your parents or other important adults in your life are unlikely to sit down on the couch some Sunday afternoon and conduct a lecture on how they feel about life and what they want for you, complete with charts, graphs and handouts. If your parents have a happy marriage, however, you have undoubtedly learned something from them. If your brother is encouraged to think about college, while you're encouraged to clean up your room or do something about your hair, you've learned something about sex roles, too. Is it more important to them that you make the honor roll, or that you have a date every Saturday night? Are there often arguments in your family? What are they usually about? What messages have your parents conveyed about the kind of work women should do? What have they told you about your own potential? Observe the way everyone in your family treats everyone else. How do you feel about that treatment?

When you were growing up, what messages or information did you receive from your mother and other adult women about the importance of the following:

Success in school? _Success in school is important for my future, I should try my best to do good in it._

Appearance? _being the most beautiful person in the world is not that important. looking clean and neat is important._

Marriage? _Intermarriges can be hard. But_ ___

Career? _take your time in choosing a career that you like._

Children? ___

When you were growing up, what messages or information did you receive from your father and other adult males about the importance of the following:

Success in school? _Successeding in school is very important. And so is college_

Appearance? _looks aren't everything as long as you look respectable._

Marriage? ___

Career? _Choose a career which you will enjoy on a long term basis._

Children? ___

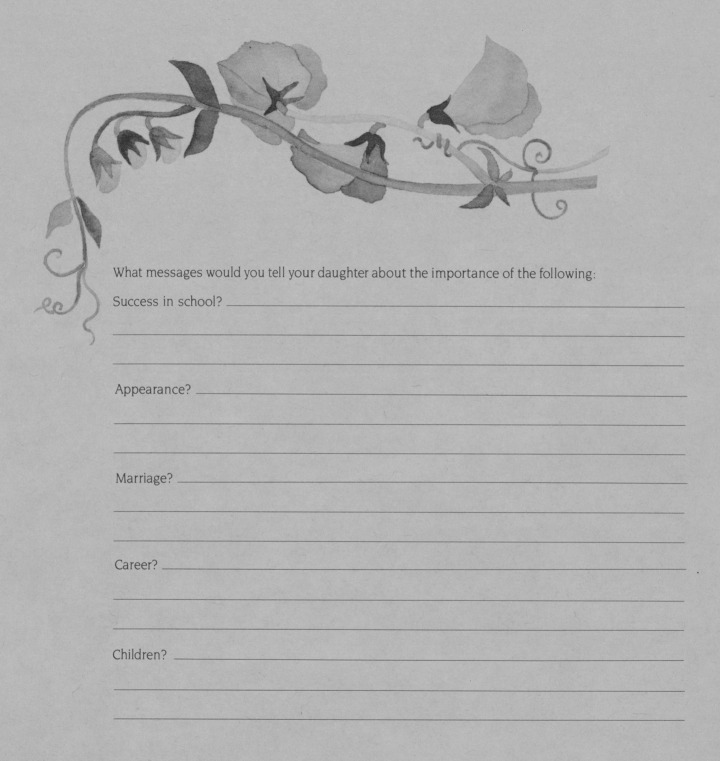

What messages would you tell your daughter about the importance of the following:

Success in school? _____
_____
_____
_____

Appearance? _____
_____
_____

Marriage? _____
_____
_____

Career? _____
_____
_____

Children? _____
_____
_____

Bridge the Generation Gap

Interview two women (your mother, another woman who is important to you, like your grandmother, a teacher you admire, or an employer). One of the women you interview should currently have a full-time job. Discover how they felt about being women as they were growing up and how they feel about the roles of women today.

PERSON I INTERVIEWED: _____

RELATIONSHIP: _____

DATE: _____

ASK THESE QUESTIONS:

Do you think girls are raised differently than boys? If so, in what ways?

_____

_____

Do you think you were treated differently because you were a girl?

_____

_____

Should young girls today prepare for a career outside the home? Why or why not?

_____

_____

If you could relive your life, what changes would you make in it?

_____

_____

Women play many important roles in their lives. Which do you think should be most important?

_____

_____

If you were going to give me one piece of advice about my future, what would it be?

_____

_____

PERSON I INTERVIEWED: _____

RELATIONSHIP: _____

DATE: _____

ASK THESE QUESTIONS:

Do you think girls are raised differently than boys? If so, in what ways?

_____

_____

Do you think you were treated differently because you were a girl?

_____

_____

Should young girls today prepare for a career? Why or why not?

_____

_____

If you could relive your life, what changes would you make in it?

_____

_____

Women play many important roles in their lives. Which do you think should be most important?

_____

_____

If you were going to give me one piece of advice, what would it be?

_____

_____

Your attitudes are influenced by what you see around you, as well as by your family.

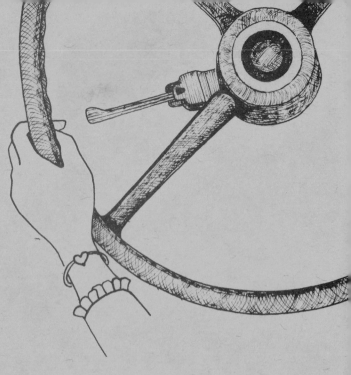

Have You Ever Met a Woman Truck Driver?

Our own observations give us much true and needed information. You may have observed, for instance, that shaking a soft drink can before you open it is not a good idea — especially inside small cars. But some of the ideas we acquire through observation are false. Because you rarely meet a woman truck driver or a male nurse, you may think that such people do not exist, or, if they do, that they are weird. That's natural. You grew up in a world in which it was "normal" for *men* to be truck drivers and *women* to be nurses. There comes a time when you must question what you see. If something is "normal," is it automatically right and proper? If it is not typical, is it necessarily wrong?

Although your feelings are not easily changed, it's important to consider why you feel as you do. By answering the following questions, you may gain some insight into your attitudes. You may even open your eyes to a whole new world of choices.

Is it right for *only* men to be truck drivers? What is there about the job that makes it unsuitable for a woman?

_____

_____

_____

Would you like to be a truck driver? Why or why not?

_____

_____

_____

Look back at what you just wrote. Were the reasons you gave based on what a truck driver actually does on the job?

_____

_____

_____

Did you know that the world is populated primarily by males, professionals, whites and members of the middle class? Did you know that women make up only 28 percent of the population; that one-half of all women are teenagers or in their early twenties; that more than one-third are unemployed or have no identifiable purpose beyond offering emotional support to men or serving as objects of sexual desire; that minorities are generally service workers, criminals, victims or students; that the elderly are usually infirm, senile, or helpless? If you watch much TV, these are the impressions you get daily on the "tube".[2]
— Dennis Coon
    Introduction to Psychology:
    Exploration and Application

Every time you watch TV or open a magazine, you learn something about what it means to be a woman. What you learn is not necessarily *true*, you understand. As the paragraph above shows, the world portrayed by television bears little resemblance to the world in which we live. Women, for example, make up 51 percent of the population in our country. They come in all sizes, shapes, and ages. In fact, women live an average of eight years longer than men. Most women in the United States work outside the home.

Although you may not realize it, the imaginary world we see on TV makes a deep impression. If, according to TV, all nurses are women and all doctors are men, you are more likely to consider a career in nursing. Or if you see a woman on TV working full time and maintaining a happy family with little or no effort, you may get the idea that being "superwoman" is very easy. In fact, you can have a high-paying career and a family, but choices will need to be made and considerable effort in balancing your many roles will be required.

Take a closer look at the images of men and women commonly created by the media. Make a collage on the next page by pasting pictures and words from magazines and newspapers which show how men and women are typically portrayed. Don't forget to consider TV and movies as well as printed materials.

Collage

What TV Tells You

Every time you watch TV you receive messages about which jobs are considered proper for women. Watch for two hours, then complete the following exercise. Repeat this activity several times during the next month, and see what pattern emerges.

SHOW	CHARACTER	SEX	ROLE OR OCCUPATION

COMMERCIAL	CHARACTER	SEX	ROLE OR OCCUPATION

What did you learn from this exercise?

What "Kid-Vid" (TV for Children) Tells You

The things you learned as a child about proper roles for girls and boys may still be influencing the way you think — and the way children today are learning to think. On Saturday morning, watch the kiddie shows and commercials. What do they tell you about differences between boys and girls? Record your observations below.

COMMERCIAL OR SHOW	CHARACTER	SEX	PRODUCT ADVERTISED OR CHARACTER'S ACTIVITY

What careers do commercials seem to encourage boys to pursue through their play?

_____

_____

What career options are shown for girls through play?

_____

_____

Have any of the advertisers shown girls playing with trucks, building materials or other "boy-oriented toys"?

Yes _____   No _____   If yes, which? _____

Have any of the advertisers shown boys playing with dolls, toy appliances or other "girl-oriented toys"?

Yes _____   No _____   If yes, which? _____

Textbooks and what you learn in school also influence your opinions. Let's look at history, the study of events and people from the past.

When you read history books, do you ever wonder where all the *women* are? You'd almost think that, until just recently, the world was inhabited almost entirely by men (who apparently were dropped here from a passing space ship, or sprouted out of the ground, like carrots). When a woman does make an appearance in history books, she usually stays just long enough to be burned at the stake or have her head chopped off.

Women, of course, have always existed. They've worked hard and played an important role in the development of our world. Women have been queens and explorers, leaders in battle, artists and musicians, writers and scientists, spies and outlaws, teachers and athletes, and just about anything else you can name. That's important for you to remember. Women may have been neglected or repressed in history books, but that doesn't mean they haven't made history.

In the next exercise, see if you can fill in the names of both men and women who have become famous for their work in each of the categories listed. If it's easier to think of men than women (and more likely it will be), remember that is partly due to the emphasis history has given men's achievements.

Women and Men in History

EXPLORERS:
Female _____ Male _____

MILITARY LEADERS:
Female _____ Male _____

MUSICAL COMPOSERS:
Female _____ Male _____

NATIONAL LEADERS (prior to 1850):
Female _____ Male _____

FAMOUS KINGS AND QUEENS (prior to 1850):
Female _____ Male _____

EARLY AMERICAN COLONIAL LEADERS:
Female _____ Male _____

CURRENT NATIONAL LEADERS:
Female _____ Male _____

INFAMOUS VILLAINS:
Female _____ Male _____

ATHLETES:
Female _____ Male _____

UNITED STATES SENATORS:
Female _____ Male _____

AUTHORS:
Female _____ Male _____

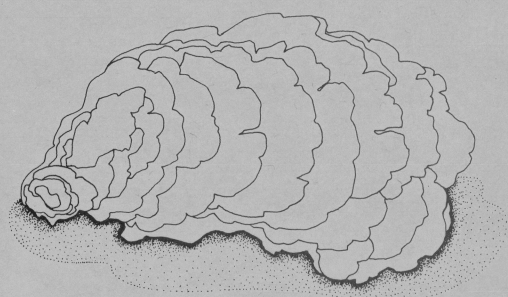

What Qualities Does a Woman Possess?

What are the characteristics of "normal" men and women? Let's examine your perceptions.

Are women typically emotional or unemotional? How about men? Do you think they are usually emotional? Or unemotional? The following exercise, based on a study called the *Broverman Scale*[3], will help you visualize the differences you perceive between the sexes. In the left hand column is one list of characteristics. Their opposites are listed in the right hand column. On the lines between, put a check mark to indicate how you would rate a typical man on that scale. For example, if you think most men are aggressive, mark the space nearest that word. If you think they are non-aggressive, mark the space at the opposite end of the scale. If you think most men rank somewhere between, mark whatever place you think is appropriate. Then go on to the second set and repeat the exercise; this time show how you think a typical woman would rate.

BROVERMAN SHORT FORM CHARACTERISTIC SCALE

This scale has seven spaces between each pair of opposing characteristics. For each pair, mark one of the seven spaces, basing your choice on which space best describes "normal" or typical males. Use the middle space only if you feel completely neutral or evenly divided.

MALE

Aggressive	___ ___ ___ ✓ ___ ___ ___	Non-aggressive
Independent	___ ___ ___ ___ ___ ___ ___	Dependent
Emotional	___ ___ ___ ___ ___ ___ ___	Unemotional
Subjective	___ ___ ___ ___ ___ ___ ___	Objective
Submissive	___ ___ ___ ___ ___ ___ ___	Dominant
Excitable	___ ___ ___ ___ ___ ___ ___	Non-excitable
Competitive	___ ___ ___ ___ ___ ___ ___	Non-competitive
Easily hurt	___ ___ ___ ___ ___ ___ ___	Not easily hurt
Adventurous	___ ___ ___ ___ ___ ___ ___	Cautious
Leader	___ ___ ___ ___ ___ ___ ___	Follower
Not appearance oriented	___ ___ ___ ___ ___ ___ ___	Appearance oriented

BROVERMAN SHORT FORM CHARACTERISTIC SCALE

This scale has seven spaces between each pair of opposing characteristics. For each pair, mark one of the seven spaces, basing your choice on which space best describes "normal" or typical females. Use the middle space only if you feel completely neutral or evenly divided.

FEMALE

Aggressive	___ ___ ___ ___ ___ ___ ___	Non-aggressive
Independent	___ ___ ___ ___ ___ ___ ___	Dependent
Emotional	___ ___ ___ ___ ___ ___ ___	Unemotional
Subjective	___ ___ ___ ___ ___ ___ ___	Objective
Submissive	___ ___ ___ ___ ___ ___ ___	Dominant
Excitable	___ ___ ___ ___ ___ ___ ___	Non-excitable
Competitive	___ ___ ___ ___ ___ ___ ___	Non-competitive
Easily hurt	___ ___ ___ ___ ___ ___ ___	Not easily hurt
Adventurous	___ ___ ___ ___ ___ ___ ___	Cautious
Leader	___ ___ ___ ___ ___ ___ ___	Follower
Not appearance oriented	___ ___ ___ ___ ___ ___ ___	Appearance oriented

How About a Healthy Adult?

Repeat the exercise again, this time rating a healthy adult. How would a well-adjusted, mature person rate on this scale?

BROVERMAN SHORT FORM CHARACTERISTIC SCALE

This scale has seven spaces between each pair of opposing characteristics. For each pair, mark one of the seven spaces, basing your choice on which space best describes "normal" healthy adults. Use the middle space only if you feel completely neutral or evenly divided.

HEALTHY ADULT

Aggressive	___ ___ ___ ___ ___ ___ ___	Non-aggressive
Independent	___ ___ ___ ___ ___ ___ ___	Dependent
Emotional	___ ___ ___ ___ ___ ___ ___	Unemotional
Subjective	___ ___ ___ ___ ___ ___ ___	Objective
Submissive	___ ___ ___ ___ ___ ___ ___	Dominant
Excitable	___ ___ ___ ___ ___ ___ ___	Non-excitable
Competitive	___ ___ ___ ___ ___ ___ ___	Non-competitive
Easily hurt	___ ___ ___ ___ ___ ___ ___	Not easily hurt
Adventurous	___ ___ ___ ___ ___ ___ ___	Cautious
Leader	___ ___ ___ ___ ___ ___ ___	Follower
Not appearance oriented	___ ___ ___ ___ ___ ___ ___	Appearance oriented

After reviewing your answers, what do you conclude about a healthy adult?

Inge and Donald Broverman and several co-workers gave 79 psychologists (46 male and 33 female) the rating scales you just completed.* The psychologists' ratings for "healthy, mature adult men" were very similar to those for "healthy adult with sex unspecified." The "healthy, mature adult woman," on the other hand, differed from both men and adults. The psychologists rated women as more submissive, more emotional, more easily influenced, more excitable in a minor crisis, more vain, more easily hurt emotionally, less objective, less independent, less adventurous, less competitive and less aggressive. To top things off, they said women exhibited a dislike of math and science.

These results show that the psychologists believed dependency, passivity, and submissiveness are normal characteristics of healthy mature women, but not of their male counterparts, *nor* of adults in general. The Brovermans' study implies that sex-role stereotyping limits healthy functioning and development.

*The rating scales used here are abbreviated.

To compare your ratings with those of classmates or friends, assign the numerical values 1, 2, 3, 4, 5, 6, and 7 to each line (left to right).

Example:

Aggressive   __1__   __2__   __3__   __4__   __5__   __6__   __7__   Non-aggressive

Add the numbers you and your group checked for each of the characteristics listed. For example, if for "aggressive — non-aggressive" the six people in your group checked the spaces 2, 2, 3, 1, 2, 2, on the page labeled "male," the average rating would be 2. (2 + 2 + 3 + 1 + 2 + 2 = 12 and 12 divided by 6 = 2.) This would show that those taking the survey think males are fairly aggressive. (An average of 4 indicates a middle score, halfway between the two extremes.) Find the average for each characteristic listed on all three tests.

Now rate *yourself*. For each pair of characteristics, mark the space you feel best indicates your personality.

Your Name _____

Aggressive	___ ___ ___ ___ ___ ___ ___	Non-aggressive
Independent	___ ___ ___ ___ ___ ___ ___	Dependent
Emotional	___ ___ ___ ___ ___ ___ ___	Unemotional
Subjective	___ ___ ___ ___ ___ ___ ___	Objective
Submissive	___ ___ ___ ___ ___ ___ ___	Dominant
Excitable	___ ___ ___ ___ ___ ___ ___	Non-excitable
Competitive	___ ___ ___ ___ ___ ___ ___	Non-competitive
Easily hurt	___ ___ ___ ___ ___ ___ ___	Not easily hurt
Adventurous	___ ___ ___ ___ ___ ___ ___	Cautious
Leader	___ ___ ___ ___ ___ ___ ___	Follower
Not appearance oriented	___ ___ ___ ___ ___ ___ ___	Appearance oriented

Do *your* characteristics differ from those you attributed to a "Healthy Adult?" If so, maybe you should consider ways you can strengthen or change your characteristics to match your feelings about what is healthy.

How do your family and friends feel about men and women? We've included another copy of the exercise so you can make copies and conduct your own test. You can't help but be affected by the feelings of those closest to you. They naturally want you to be a mature and happy person. Yet without meaning to, they may be sending you — and themselves — the wrong kinds of messages about what is proper or appropriate behavior. If they are, they may be just as surprised to learn it as you were!

BROVERMAN SHORT FORM CHARACTERISTIC SCALE

This scale has seven spaces between each pair of opposing characteristics. For each pair, mark one of the seven spaces, basing your choice on which space best describes "normal" or typical males. Use the middle space only if you feel completely neutral or evenly divided.

MALE

Aggressive	___ ___ ___ ___ ___ ___ ___	Non-aggressive
Independent	___ ___ ___ ___ ___ ___ ___	Dependent
Emotional	___ ___ ___ ___ ___ ___ ___	Unemotional
Subjective	___ ___ ___ ___ ___ ___ ___	Objective
Submissive	___ ___ ___ ___ ___ ___ ___	Dominant
Excitable	___ ___ ___ ___ ___ ___ ___	Non-excitable
Competitive	___ ___ ___ ___ ___ ___ ___	Non-competitive
Easily hurt	___ ___ ___ ___ ___ ___ ___	Not easily hurt
Adventurous	___ ___ ___ ___ ___ ___ ___	Cautious
Leader	___ ___ ___ ___ ___ ___ ___	Follower
Not appearance oriented	___ ___ ___ ___ ___ ___ ___	Appearance oriented

BROVERMAN SHORT FORM CHARACTERISTIC SCALE

This scale has seven spaces between each pair of opposing characteristics. For each pair, mark one of the seven spaces, basing your choice on which space best describes "normal" or typical females. Use the middle space only if you feel completely neutral or evenly divided.

FEMALE

Aggressive	___ ___ ___ ___ ___ ___ ___	Non-aggressive
Independent	___ ___ ___ ___ ___ ___ ___	Dependent
Emotional	___ ___ ___ ___ ___ ___ ___	Unemotional
Subjective	___ ___ ___ ___ ___ ___ ___	Objective
Submissive	___ ___ ___ ___ ___ ___ ___	Dominant
Excitable	___ ___ ___ ___ ___ ___ ___	Non-excitable
Competitive	___ ___ ___ ___ ___ ___ ___	Non-competitive
Easily hurt	___ ___ ___ ___ ___ ___ ___	Not easily hurt
Adventurous	___ ___ ___ ___ ___ ___ ___	Cautious
Leader	___ ___ ___ ___ ___ ___ ___	Follower
Not appearance oriented	___ ___ ___ ___ ___ ___ ___	Appearance oriented

BROVERMAN SHORT FORM CHARACTERISTIC SCALE

This scale has seven spaces between each pair of opposing characteristics. For each pair, mark one of the seven spaces, basing your choice on which space best describes "normal" healthy adults. Use the middle space only if you feel completely neutral or evenly divided.

HEALTHY ADULT

Aggressive	___	___	___	___	___	___	___	Non-aggressive
Independent	___	___	___	___	___	___	___	Dependent
Emotional	___	___	___	___	___	___	___	Unemotional
Subjective	___	___	___	___	___	___	___	Objective
Submissive	___	___	___	___	___	___	___	Dominant
Excitable	___	___	___	___	___	___	___	Non-excitable
Competitive	___	___	___	___	___	___	___	Non-competitive
Easily hurt	___	___	___	___	___	___	___	Not easily hurt
Adventurous	___	___	___	___	___	___	___	Cautious
Leader	___	___	___	___	___	___	___	Follower
Not appearance oriented	___	___	___	___	___	___	___	Appearance oriented

You'll find a page entitled ``Reflections'' at the end of each chapter.
Use it to jot down your thoughts and feelings about what you've just
learned. Or, use it for poetry, artwork, snapshots or whatever is
meaningful to you.

REFLECTIONS

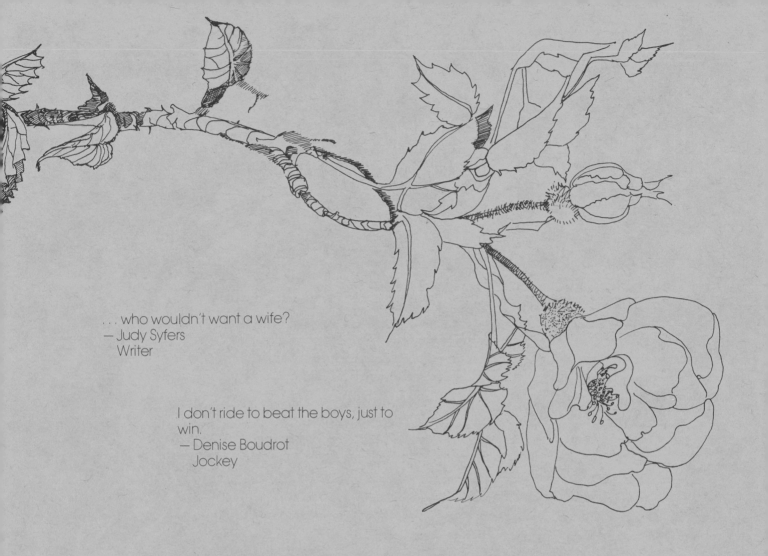

. . . who wouldn't want a wife?
— Judy Syfers
Writer

I don't ride to beat the boys, just to win.
— Denise Boudrot
Jockey

CHAPTER TWO
Being a Woman
Isn't Always Easy

Greater awareness can help you handle choices

It's Okay for Girls to Want a Career

Betty Sue's Story

Betty Sue was extremely concerned about her femininity. She had thirteen sweaters in various shades of pink, batted her long, expertly-applied eyelashes constantly, and had perfected a giggle that made some people want to slug her right behind her delicately scented, sea shell-like little ears. Of course, no one ever did it because Betty Sue looked as if she would shatter like crystal at the slightest touch.

When she was eighteen, Betty Sue married a man who owned a construction company. Betty Sue's husband supplied her with buckets of perfume, closets full of satin negligees and high-heeled slippers, and every shade of nail polish Revlon produced. Then suddenly, her husband was killed in an airplane crash. At first Betty Sue didn't know what to do. She soon made a courageous decision. She would take over her husband's business. Everyone laughed, saying she'd change her mind as soon as she broke her first fingernail. Betty Sue surprised them all. She learned to operate heavy equipment, to read plans, to bid on jobs, to hire, fire, and negotiate with unions; and she made the company more successful than ever before.

How did Betty Sue feel about her "new self"? Whenever anyone asked if she felt badly about appearing unfeminine, she said, "This is what feminine looks like."

Somewhere along the road, the meaning of the word "feminine" has become confused. It doesn't mean weak or helpless or dumb. It simply means belonging to the female sex.

Since you are female, anything you do — or are capable of doing — may be considered "feminine." Of course the roles of wife and mother are traditionally feminine. Being a truck driver, mechanic, doctor, or physicist, can be just as feminine, simply because women have already proved that they are capable of such work.

Just as you'll hear many misconceptions about what a woman *should be*, there are also many silly notions about what women *can do*. After all, what would we do if there were a national crisis and the president were getting her legs waxed at Elizabeth Arden's? Could a woman be an airline pilot? How silly. Everyone knows she'd burst into tears and give up if she ran into a thunderstorm over Indianapolis! Does this sound ridiculous? It *is* ridiculous. Just the same there are still people around who think that way. Don't *you* be one of them. Putting irrational limits on your aspirations will only make you feel less worthy as a person, and it will *cost you money*.

The Working World

"When I grow up, I want to be a _____." You can usually tell the sex of a person by the way he or she completes that sentence. Why? When you look at the working world today, most occupations are still dominated by one sex or the other. Below is a list of jobs. Read through it and put an F by jobs usually held by women, and an M by those jobs usually held by men. At this point in your journal we hope you are saying to yourself, "I don't see jobs as either male or female." For this exercise though, consider how the world is today.

What do you see when you walk into a hospital? You see doctors M, and nurses F. Likewise, most secretaries are women. Put an F by secretary. When you walk into a bank, what do you see? It's tellers F and bank officers M.

Keep in mind that, just because a pattern exists, there is no reason for you to assume that it is carved in stone. Changes are taking place in all fields.

_____ Architect	_____ Elementary school teacher
_____ Telephone installer	_____ Carpenter
_____ Engineer	_____ Painter (construction)
_____ Clerk-typist	_____ Air traffic controller
_____ Bookkeeper	_____ Airplane mechanic
_____ Secretary	_____ Pilot
_____ Computer programmer	_____ Flight attendant
_____ Dental assistant	_____ Truck driver
_____ Bank teller	_____ Nurse
_____ Mail carrier	_____ Doctor
_____ Lawyer	_____ Receptionist

Now.let's attach salaries to these jobs. The salaries given below are from the 1986-87 *Occupational Outlook Handbook* published by the U.S. Department of Labor. These figures represent the average salary based on 1984-1985 surveys.

Using the figures listed, complete a graph of salaries on the following page. Use a *pen* for each dot that represents a "woman's job" as identified by the symbol F. Use a *pencil* for each dot that represents a "man's job" as identified by the symbol M. Connect the pencil dots with pencil and the pen dots with pen. (Colored pens or pencils may be used instead of plain pens and pencils.)

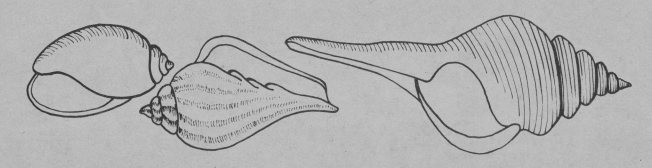

AVERAGE ANNUAL SALARIES

Architect	$29,000
Telephone installer	$27,000
Engineer	$41,000
Typist	$15,000
Bookkeeper	$13,500
Secretary	$17,000
Computer Programmer	$26,000
Dental Assistant	$12,000
Bank Teller	$11,000
Lawyer	$88,000
Mail Carrier	$25,000
Elementary School Teacher	$23,000
Carpenter	$25,000
Painter (Houses)	$16,000
Air Traffic Controller	$35,000
Airplane Mechanic	$25,000
Pilot	$80,000
Flight Attendant	$23,000
Truck Driver (Long Distance)	$25,000
Nurse	$21,000
Doctor	$108,000
Receptionist	$14,000

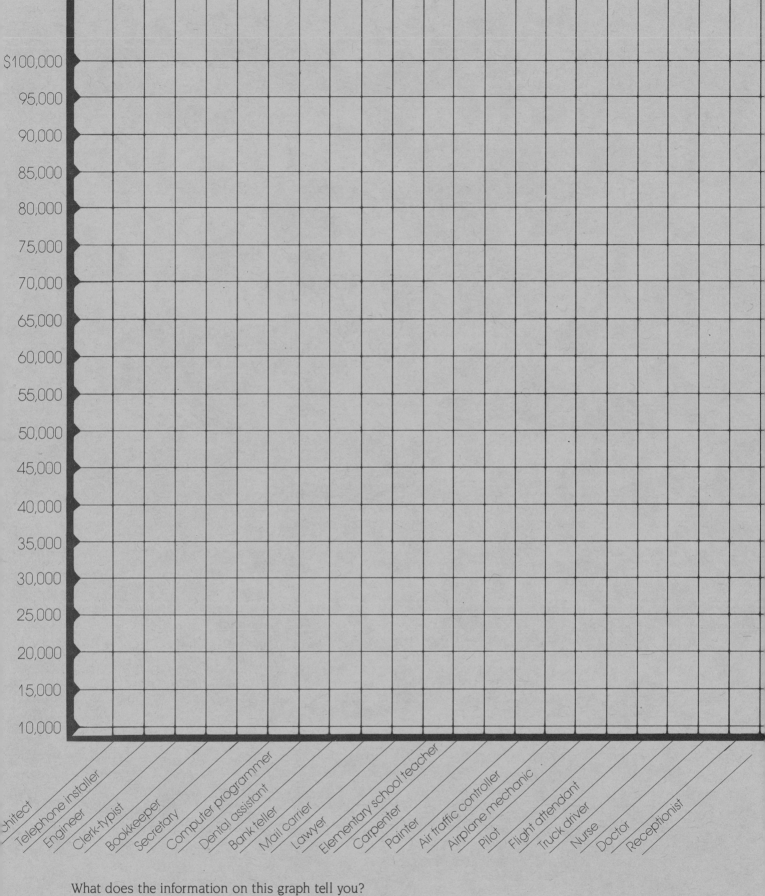

$100,000
95,000
90,000
85,000
80,000
75,000
70,000
65,000
60,000
55,000
50,000
45,000
40,000
35,000
30,000
25,000
20,000
15,000
10,000

Architect · Telephone installer · Engineer · Clerk-typist · Bookkeeper · Secretary · Computer programmer · Dental assistant · Bank teller · Mail carrier · Lawyer · Elementary school teacher · Carpenter · Painter · Air traffic controller · Airplane mechanic · Pilot · Flight attendant · Truck driver · Nurse · Doctor · Receptionist

What does the information on this graph tell you?

_____

_____

39

One must be chary of words
because they turn into cages.
— Viola Spolin

Are You Limiting Your Choices?

If you're good with numbers, why shouldn't you consider being an accountant instead of a bookkeeper? If you're interested in medicine, why immediately presume that you have to be a nurse? This is the time for you to explore and to dream. What would you want to be if you were a boy? As a girl is there any *real* reason why you shouldn't be the same thing? Why should your sex stand in the way of becoming anything you want to be?

COMMENTS:

_____

_____

_____

_____

_____

_____

_____

_____

_____

_____

_____

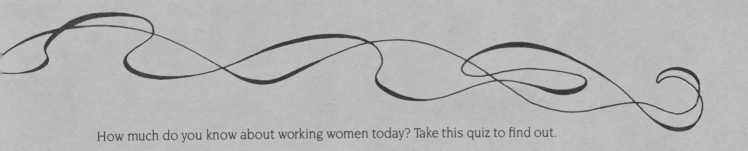

How much do you know about working women today? Take this quiz to find out.

WOMEN IN THE WORKFORCE

1. The number of women who work for pay at some time during their lives is
   a. 3 out of 10
   b. 5 out of 10
   c. 7 out of 10
   d. 9 out of 10

2. In 1985 the percentage of women who worked because of economic need (self-supporting or husband earned less than $15,000) was
   a. 33 percent
   b. 45 percent
   c. 56 percent
   d. 67 percent

3. Married men with non-working wives, and one or more children, make up what percentage of all households?
   a. 9.9 percent
   b. 26.4 percent
   c. 62.8 percent
   d. 79.3 percent

4. Women make up what percentage of the total workforce?
   a. 15 percent
   b. 24 percent
   c. 44 percent
   d. 50 percent

5. In 1984, the median earnings for men and women who worked full-time, year-round were
   a. men — $26,456,   women — $24,954
   b. men — $23,218,   women — $14,780
   c. men — $22,317,   women — $19,942
   d. men — $20,561,   women — $20,240

6. In the past decade, three-fifths of the labor force increase has been among
   a. women
   b. minority women
   c. minorities
   d. married women

7. In 1985, fully employed, female high school graduates (with no college background) earned
   a. more than male high school graduates
   b. less than men who did not complete elementary school
   c. more than male high school graduates, but less than male college graduates
   d. about the same as male high school graduates

8. The absentee rate from work for women is
   a. much greater than for men
   b. slightly more than for men
   c. much less than for men
   d. slightly less than for men

9. The unemployment rate of minority women, compared to that of Caucasian women, is
   a. about the same
   b. less than the rate for Caucasian women
   c. 35 percent more
   d. twice as high

10. The average woman worker will work outside the home between _____ in her lifetime
    a. 5-10 years
    b. 10-15 years
    c. 15-20 years
    d. 20-40 years

Answers follow.

ANSWERS[4]

1. The number of women who work for pay some time during their lives is:
   (d) nine out of ten.

2. The percentage of women, who worked because of economic need in 1985 was:
   (d) 67 percent. Most women work because they have to work. The myth that women work only to amuse themselves, or to buy luxuries for their families, is a very limiting one because it is used to justify keeping women in low-paying jobs.

3. Married men with non-working wives and one or more children in 1985 made up:
   (a) 9.9 percent of all households. Families are changing rapidly in today's society. The high divorce rate is creating many single-parent families. Also, many people are choosing not to have any children or to remain single.

4. Women make up:
   (c) 44 percent of the total workforce.

5. In 1984 the median earnings for men and women who worked full time were:
   (b) men-$23,218, women-$14,780. The gap between the earnings of men and women is narrowing very slowly. Many explanations for the gap are given, but one of the most prominent reasons is that women are concentrated in low-paying jobs. For example, secretaries, who are usually women, make much less than construction workers, who are mostly men.

6. In the past decade, three-fifths of the labor force increase has been among
   (a) women. Women from all backgrounds are entering the workforce.

7. In 1985 fully employed women high school graduates (with no college background) earned:
   (b) less than men who did not complete elementary school. If you look back to the graph you completed earlier on page 39, you will see the large difference in the pay for traditional men's jobs versus traditional women's jobs. Notice that jobs such as house painter and truck driver are relatively high-salaried jobs even though they require little education. Construction or farm jobs often require apprenticeship or on-the-job training, rather than formal education.

8. The absentee rate from work for women is:
   (b) slightly more than for men. The rates are 5.6 days a year for women and 5.2 days a year for men. This question was included to show that women are not more likely to be absent from work than men. (The statement that women are likely to be sick often is sometimes used as an excuse for not hiring women.)

9. The unemployment rate for minority women, compared to that of Caucasian women, is:
   (d) twice as much.

10. The average female worker will work between:
    (d) 20 to 40 years in her lifetime. Those women who expect to work only a short period of time may be in for some surprises.

DOONESBURY

by Garry Trudeau

REFLECTIONS

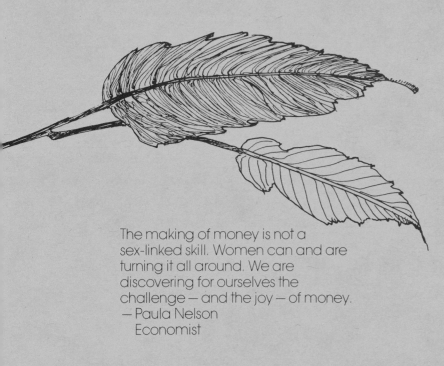

The making of money is not a
sex-linked skill. Women can and are
turning it all around. We are
discovering for ourselves the
challenge — and the joy — of money.
— Paula Nelson
    Economist

CHAPTER THREE

The High Cost
of Living

Could you support a family
on your income alone?

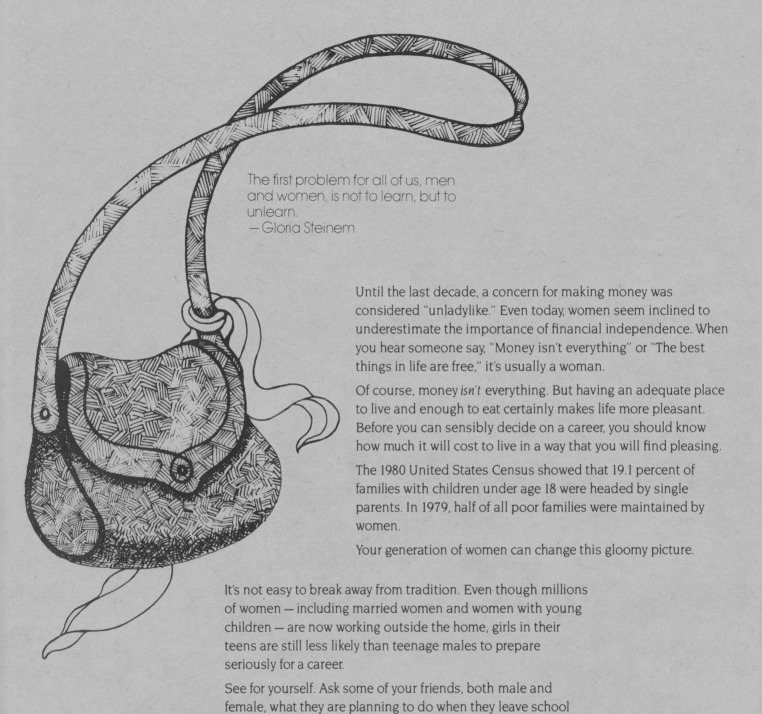

The first problem for all of us, men and women, is not to learn, but to unlearn.
— Gloria Steinem

Until the last decade, a concern for making money was considered "unladylike." Even today, women seem inclined to underestimate the importance of financial independence. When you hear someone say, "Money isn't everything" or "The best things in life are free," it's usually a woman.

Of course, money *isn't* everything. But having an adequate place to live and enough to eat certainly makes life more pleasant. Before you can sensibly decide on a career, you should know how much it will cost to live in a way that you will find pleasing.

The 1980 United States Census showed that 19.1 percent of families with children under age 18 were headed by single parents. In 1979, half of all poor families were maintained by women.

Your generation of women can change this gloomy picture.

It's not easy to break away from tradition. Even though millions of women — including married women and women with young children — are now working outside the home, girls in their teens are still less likely than teenage males to prepare seriously for a career.

See for yourself. Ask some of your friends, both male and female, what they are planning to do when they leave school and what they think they might be doing when they are 30 years old. Be sure to interview both young men and young women.

Interviews

Name _____ Age _____ M or F _____

What are you planning to do after high school? _____

_____

_____

_____

What do you think you will be doing at age 30?

_____

_____

_____

Name _____ Age _____ M or F _____

What are you planning to do after high school? _____

_____

_____

_____

What do you think you will be doing at age 30?

_____

_____

_____

Name _____ Age _____ M or F _____

What are you planning to do after high school? _____

_____

_____

_____

What do you think you will be doing at age 30?

_____

_____

_____

Name _____ Age _____ M or F _____

What are you planning to do after high school? _____

_____

_____

_____

What do you think you will be doing at age 30?

_____

_____

_____

Name _____ Age _____ M or F _____

What are you planning to do after high school? _____

_____

_____

_____

What do you think you will be doing at age 30?

_____

_____

_____

Name _____ Age _____ M or F _____

What are you planning to do after high school? _____

_____

_____

_____

What do you think you will be doing at age 30?

_____

_____

_____

Do you see patterns emerging for the young men and young women? If so, what are they?

True Stories: Could This Happen to You?

Remember, we're all in this alone.
— Lily Tomlin

You see "The Happily Ever After Story" dozens of times a week on TV. There may be a few problems and a few hilarious complications, but by the end of the hour, the hero says something witty or romantic, the heroine falls into his arms, the music swells and the credits begin to roll. Unfortunately, life does not come equipped with background music, a laugh track, or even a script. Anything can happen.

You may plan to become a full-time wife and mother who is supported by a husband. Just the same, your future will be more secure if you have the ability to support yourself, should the need arise. The following stories represent only a few of the situations for women today. Read them, and then jot down your reactions to the circumstances described. Indicate how common you think the situations are.

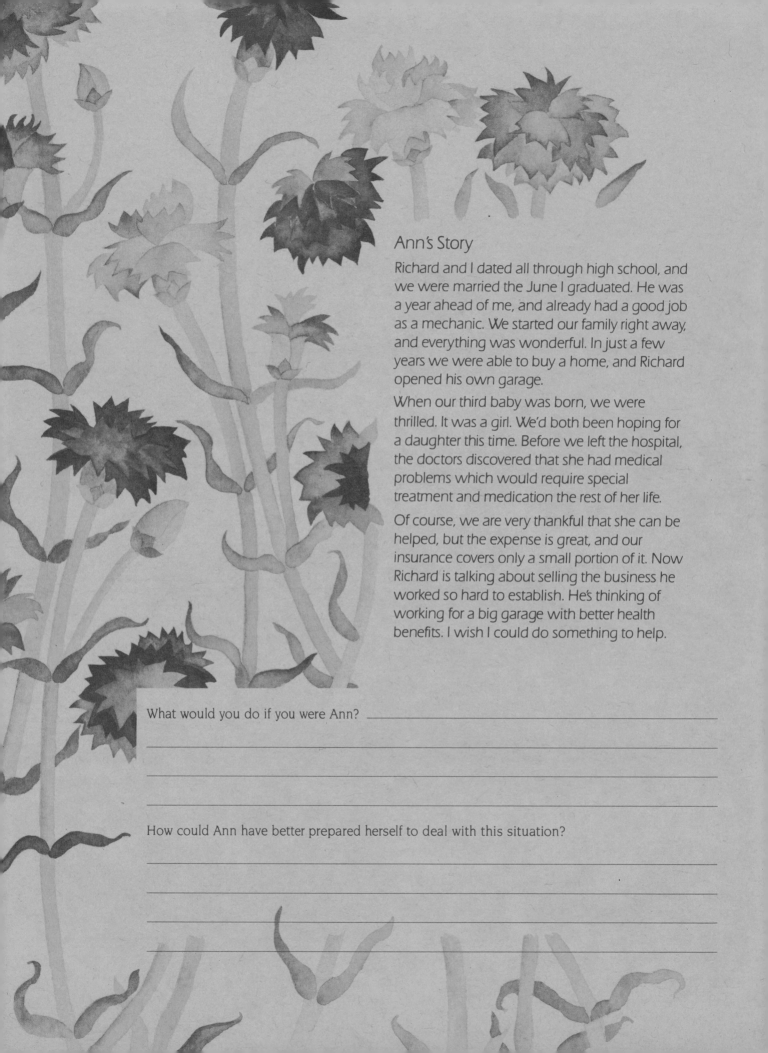

Ann's Story

Richard and I dated all through high school, and we were married the June I graduated. He was a year ahead of me, and already had a good job as a mechanic. We started our family right away, and everything was wonderful. In just a few years we were able to buy a home, and Richard opened his own garage.

When our third baby was born, we were thrilled. It was a girl. We'd both been hoping for a daughter this time. Before we left the hospital, the doctors discovered that she had medical problems which would require special treatment and medication the rest of her life.

Of course, we are very thankful that she can be helped, but the expense is great, and our insurance covers only a small portion of it. Now Richard is talking about selling the business he worked so hard to establish. He's thinking of working for a big garage with better health benefits. I wish I could do something to help.

What would you do if you were Ann? _____

_____

_____

_____

How could Ann have better prepared herself to deal with this situation?

_____

_____

_____

_____

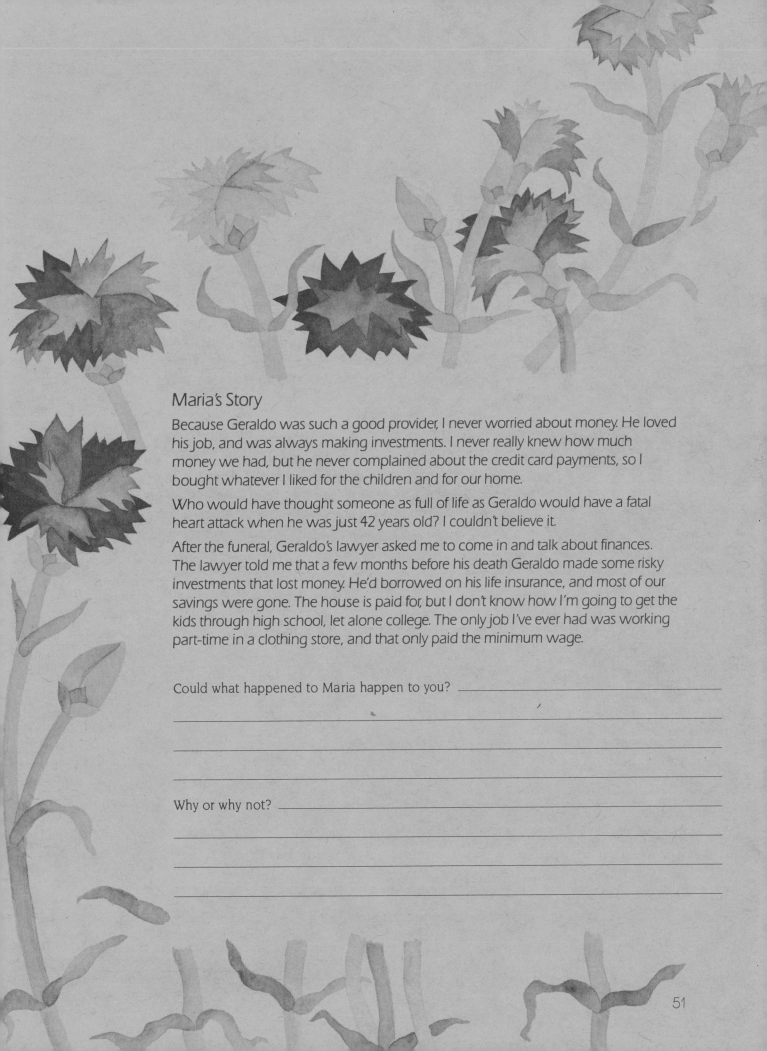

Maria's Story

Because Geraldo was such a good provider, I never worried about money. He loved his job, and was always making investments. I never really knew how much money we had, but he never complained about the credit card payments, so I bought whatever I liked for the children and for our home.

Who would have thought someone as full of life as Geraldo would have a fatal heart attack when he was just 42 years old? I couldn't believe it.

After the funeral, Geraldo's lawyer asked me to come in and talk about finances. The lawyer told me that a few months before his death Geraldo made some risky investments that lost money. He'd borrowed on his life insurance, and most of our savings were gone. The house is paid for, but I don't know how I'm going to get the kids through high school, let alone college. The only job I've ever had was working part-time in a clothing store, and that only paid the minimum wage.

Could what happened to Maria happen to you? _____

_____

_____

_____

Why or why not? _____

_____

_____

_____

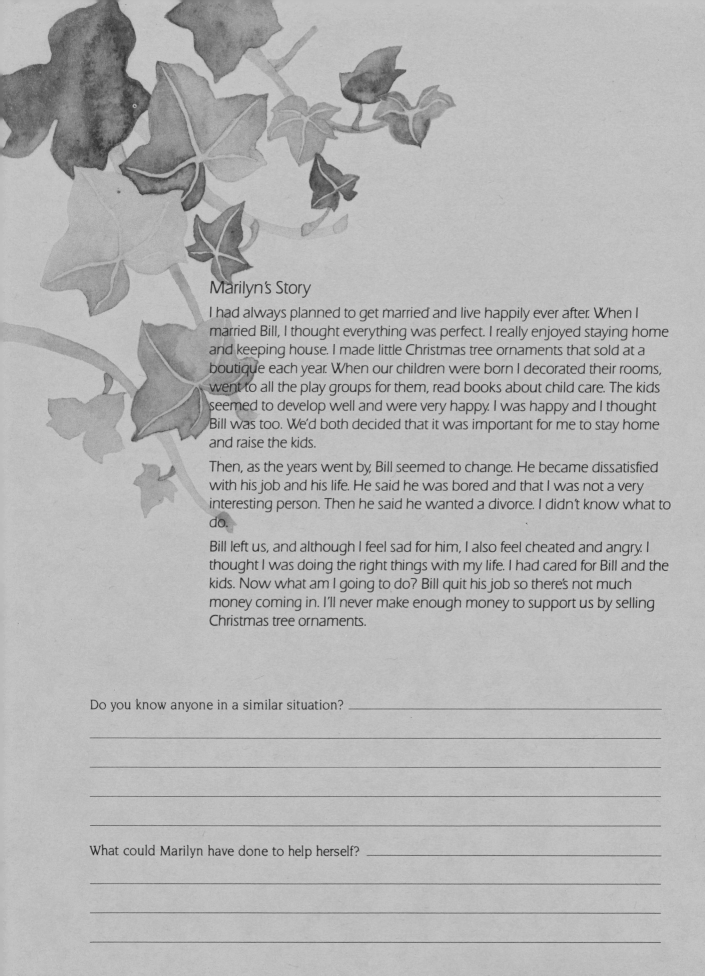

Marilyn's Story

I had always planned to get married and live happily ever after. When I married Bill, I thought everything was perfect. I really enjoyed staying home and keeping house. I made little Christmas tree ornaments that sold at a boutique each year. When our children were born I decorated their rooms, went to all the play groups for them, read books about child care. The kids seemed to develop well and were very happy. I was happy and I thought Bill was too. We'd both decided that it was important for me to stay home and raise the kids.

Then, as the years went by, Bill seemed to change. He became dissatisfied with his job and his life. He said he was bored and that I was not a very interesting person. Then he said he wanted a divorce. I didn't know what to do.

Bill left us, and although I feel sad for him, I also feel cheated and angry. I thought I was doing the right things with my life. I had cared for Bill and the kids. Now what am I going to do? Bill quit his job so there's not much money coming in. I'll never make enough money to support us by selling Christmas tree ornaments.

Do you know anyone in a similar situation? _____

_____

_____

_____

_____

What could Marilyn have done to help herself? _____

_____

_____

_____

Tracy's Story

I was a good student in high school and chose to go to a major university. I majored in English because it was fun for me. I liked reading literature, writing, and discussing ideas. College was an exciting time, and I made many friends, including my husband John. We were married right after I graduated. John earned a degree in business administration and started work with a restaurant chain. He worked his way up to a management position; everything was going well for us. We had two children, a nice house, and I was an active community volunteer.

Last year another company bought out the restaurant chain John worked for, and brought in its own management people. John is having a hard time finding another position. We're behind in our house payments and may lose our home. I wish I could get a reasonable job to help make ends meet. I never thought about having to work to earn money.

Do you know anyone in a similar situation?

_____

_____

_____

_____

Could this happen to you? _____

_____

_____

_____

_____

Why or why not? _____

_____

_____

_____

_____

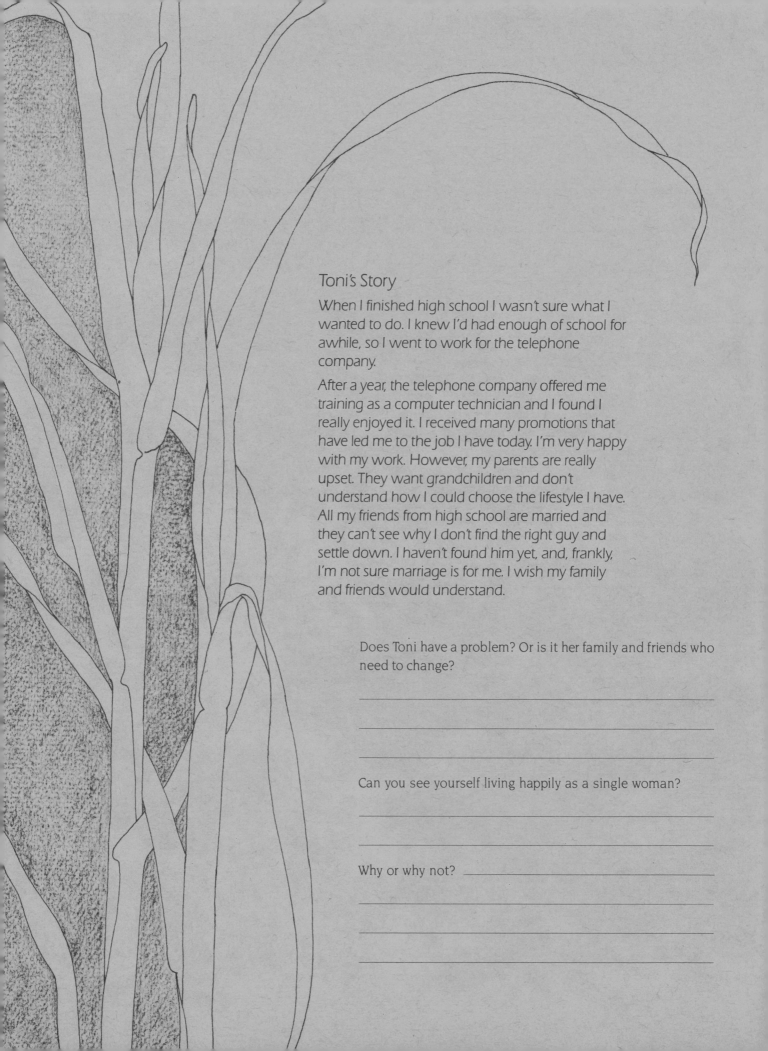

Toni's Story

When I finished high school I wasn't sure what I wanted to do. I knew I'd had enough of school for awhile, so I went to work for the telephone company.

After a year, the telephone company offered me training as a computer technician and I found I really enjoyed it. I received many promotions that have led me to the job I have today. I'm very happy with my work. However, my parents are really upset. They want grandchildren and don't understand how I could choose the lifestyle I have. All my friends from high school are married and they can't see why I don't find the right guy and settle down. I haven't found him yet, and, frankly, I'm not sure marriage is for me. I wish my family and friends would understand.

Does Toni have a problem? Or is it her family and friends who need to change?

_____

_____

_____

Can you see yourself living happily as a single woman?

_____

_____

Why or why not? _____

_____

_____

_____

Think of the women you know. Have any faced problems similar to the ones you've just examined? What decisions have these women had to make? What actions have they taken?

Write one of their stories in the space below.

If possible, interview that person and write from her point of view.

_____'s story:

_____

_____

_____

_____

_____

_____

_____

_____

_____

_____

_____

_____

_____

_____

_____

No one knows what the future holds. Expectations don't always materialize. If your expectations of a bright, secure future are to be fulfilled, it's important for you to be aware of your options for achieving that bright future. Great expectations for the future should include several possible paths to security and happiness.

It's important to have a plan for supporting yourself. Before you can make that plan, you should know how much money you must have to meet your needs. In this exercise, you will be asked to make up a detailed budget.

When you write your budget, assume that you are age 28 and supporting yourself. Look back at the exercise, "Your Life — Present and Future Visions." If you expect to have children in your twenties, assume that you now have them. List their sex and approximate ages below.

Number of children ____

Sex(es) ____ ____ ____ ____

Age(s) ____ ____ ____ ____

This exercise will take a bit of research. You won't be able to predict exactly how much something will cost, but you can estimate. Some prices can be found by looking through the classified ads of your local newspaper (especially prices for houses, apartments, cars). Friends or family members should be able to supply you with prices for such things as groceries, utilities, and insurance. You probably already know how much clothing and some other items cost.

You'll find space to paste in sample ads and bills. These pages will be fun for your family to review in future years.

YOU MAY BE TEMPTED TO SKIP THIS EXERCISE.
DON'T!
IT'S VERY IMPORTANT.

1. Housing

Whether or not you expect to have an apartment in the city, a suburban home, or a cabin in the country, housing will probably be your biggest single expense. To help you determine housing costs, let's compare monthly rental payments and the costs for purchasing a house. Then you can select one or the other. We will begin with a rental.

To select an apartment or home to rent, decide what your requirements will be at age 28 (number of bedrooms, location, pets accepted, and so forth). Then check the "Apartments for Rent" or "Homes for Rent" section of the classified ads in a newspaper. Compare features and prices before selecting one you think you would like.

In the space below, paste in two or three classified ads offering housing that might be suitable. Circle the monthly payment listed.

BUYING A HOME

If you are considering buying a home, turn to "Houses for Sale" in the classified advertisement section of a newspaper. A house of your own will be more expensive than an apartment. However, houses offer many advantages, such as having a home of your own, tax benefits, and a long-term investment. Pick out several houses in different price ranges that appeal to you. Cut out these ads and paste them below, circling the listed selling price.

Houses are very expensive items today. When, and if, you buy one, you will find that, like most people, you will not have enough cash to pay the full price. Almost no one does. Because of the huge cost, buying a house requires a very different procedure than ordinary purchases. Let's say you want to buy a record album. To do so, you merely choose your record, pay for it, and take it home. With a house, you begin by saving well in advance toward an initial payment on the house. This money is called a down payment. It is usually about 20 percent of the purchase price. For example, for a $60,000 house you would have to pay $12,000 cash as a down payment. ($60,000 × .20 = $12,000)

To obtain the rest of the money you will need to get a loan from a bank. This loan is called a mortgage. The bank will pay the seller the full price of the house (minus the down payment). You in turn must pay the bank monthly for a period of years. It often takes 30 years for a house loan to be repaid. The bank will charge you a fee known as interest for lending you its money.

For this exercise, figure out what your monthly payment would be on one of the houses you have chosen. To do so, work through the procedures given in the next section. First read the procedure, including the example. Then, using the purchase price of the house you have chosen, insert the proper figures in the blanks provided. When you are finished you will have found the amount of your monthly payment. This tells you what it would cost you to live in the house. You can then compare the cost of buying a house with the cost of renting, and choose one or the other.

FINDING MONTHLY PAYMENTS
WHEN BUYING A HOUSE

1. Multiply the purchase price of your house by 20% (.20). The answer is the down payment you'll have to pay.
2. Subtract the down payment from the purchase price. This gives you the amount you will need to borrow from the bank; that is, the amount of your loan.

Remember we said the bank will charge you a fee called interest for loaning you its money. Since this will be a major part of your monthly payment, you must figure the interest cost to find your total monthly payment. The bank does this by figuring out the number of thousands there are in your loan (dividing your loan by 1,000). For example, a $40,000 loan equals 40,000 ÷ 1,000, or 40 thousands. When a borrower agrees to a loan, the bank states the interest rate it will charge. The bank then computes the monthly payment using a standard table which lists the cost for each $1,000 of loan at different interest rates.

Look at the following table.

MONTHLY COST PER $1,000 OF LOAN

Rate of Interest	Dollars to be Paid for Each $1,000 Loan
8%	$ 7.34 for each $1,000
9%	$ 8.05 for each $1,000
10%	$ 8.78 for each $1,000
11%	$ 9.52 for each $1,000
12%	$10.29 for each $1,000
13%	$11.06 for each $1,000
14%	$11.85 for each $1,000
15%	$12.68 for each $1,000

Let's say you have a loan at 11 percent interest. This table states that, *every month* you will have to pay $9.52 multiplied by the number of thousands in the loan.

EXAMPLE:
For a $40,000 loan at 11% interest, the payment would be:

40 x $9.52 = $381 per month.

When a borrower agrees to the loan, the bank states the interest rate it will charge.

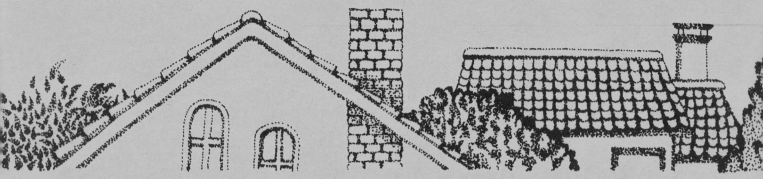

To continue your calculation,

3. Divide the amount of the loan by 1,000. This provides the number of thousands in the loan.

4. Choose an interest rate from the chart. (In reality you must pay the rate the bank asks based on current loan rates.)

5. Multiply the dollars to be paid per thousand, by the number of thousands in the loan. This gives the total monthly payment.

Now here's an example of the whole procedure.

EXAMPLE:

Beautiful three-bedroom, one-bath house on large lot. Close to shopping and schools. Good financing. $100,000. Call 654-8324.

Purchase price	$100,000
Multiplied by 20%	x .20
Equals down payment	$ 20,000
Amount of loan equals $100,000 minus $20,000	$ 80,000

There are 80 thousands in $80,000, (80,000 ÷ 1,000). If your interest rate is 11 percent, multiply the rate per thousand shown in the table for 11 percent. That is 9.52 times 80, which is the number of thousands in your loan.

Amount per thousand	$ 9.52
Multiplied by 80	x 80
Equals monthly payment	$761.60

Okay, now it is time for you to try it.

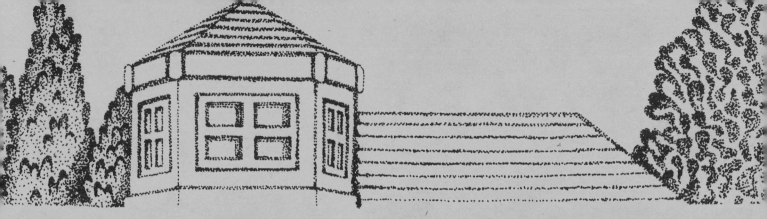

The purchase price of the home I would like to buy is $_____.

1. Multiply the purchase price by .20 to get the down payment.

    Purchase price $ _____

    Multiplied by 20%   x   .20

    Equals down payment $ _____

2. Subtract down payment from the
    purchase price.

    Purchase price $ _____

    Minus down payment $ _____

    Equals loan $ _____

3. Divide the amount of your loan by 1,000.

    Loan $ _____

    Divided by 1,000   ÷ 1,000

    Equals number of
    thousands   _____

4. Choose an amount from the interest rate
    table on page 59.

    At _____% interest the amount per thousand is _____.

5. Multiply the amount per $1,000 by the
    number of thousands in your loan.

    Amount per thousand $ _____

    Multiplied by
    number of thousands   _____

    EQUALS MONTHLY PAYMENT $ _____

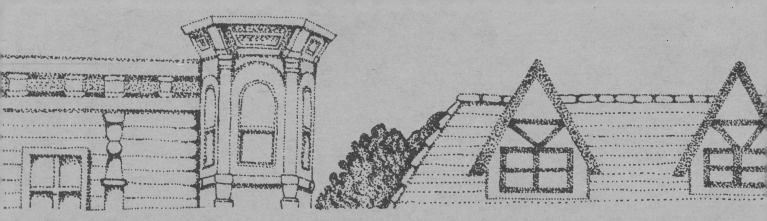

Now we've figured the cost of buying a home, right? Not yet! There are two other costs we must add. These are taxes and homeowner's insurance — neither of which renters have to pay.

Every state collects property taxes from homeowners. An approximate tax, using California as an example, is 1 percent of the assessed value. "Assessed value" refers to the amount the state thinks your house is worth. When you buy a house, the assessed value is usually the same as the purchase price. To figure your monthly taxes, multiply the purchase price by 1 percent; or find your state's formula for charging property taxes.

Purchase price $ _____

Multiplied by 1%   _____ x .01
or your state's multiple

Equals yearly property tax $ _____

To find monthly cost, divide yearly
property tax by 12.

Taxes $ _____ per month.

When you get a home loan, the bank will require you to have homeowner's insurance. Some sample yearly insurance payments (known as premiums) are listed below. Find the premium that is closest to the purchase price you chose, and divide the yearly premium by 12. This will tell you how much your insurance will actually cost each month, even though it's not paid by the month.

SAMPLE YEARLY PREMIUMS
($100 deductible coverage)

$ 80,000 - $234/year
$ 90,000 - $268/year
$100,000 - $300/year
$120,000 - $359/year
$150,000 - $444/year

Homeowner's Insurance $ _____ per month.

Your monthly homeowner's expenses will be:

Monthly payment $ _____

Monthly property taxes $ _____

Monthly homeowner's insurance $ _____

TOTAL MONTHLY COST OF A HOUSE
(Add payment, taxes,
and insurance.) $ _____

Your monthly payment for the apartment you are considering would be:

MONTHLY RENT $ _____

Do you choose the apartment to rent or the house to buy? Write your choice below. What are the reasons for your choice?

_____

_____

_____

_____

_____

_____

_____

_____

_____

_____

_____

_____

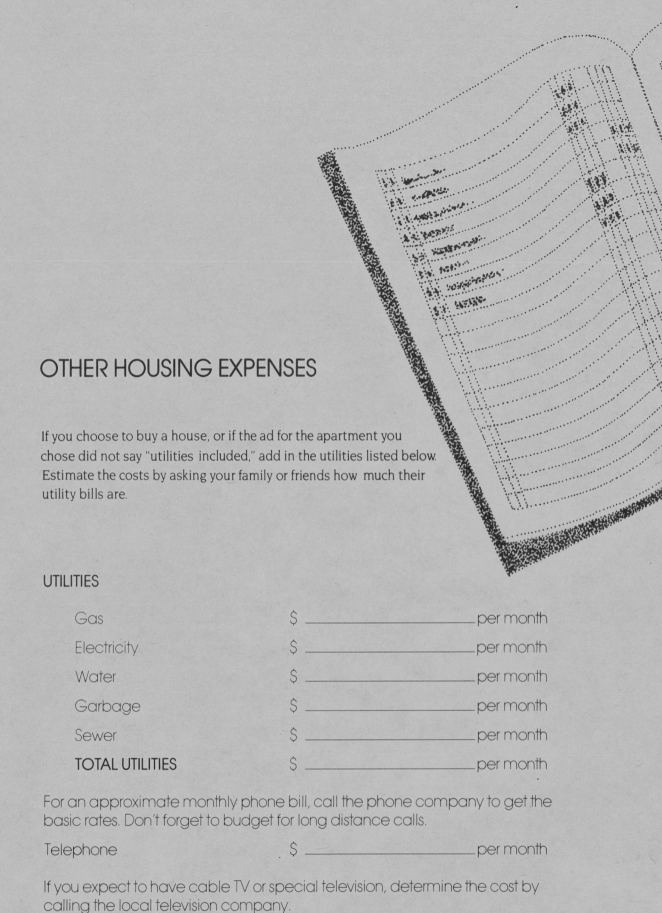

OTHER HOUSING EXPENSES

If you choose to buy a house, or if the ad for the apartment you chose did not say "utilities included," add in the utilities listed below. Estimate the costs by asking your family or friends how much their utility bills are.

UTILITIES

Gas	$ _____	per month
Electricity	$ _____	per month
Water	$ _____	per month
Garbage	$ _____	per month
Sewer	$ _____	per month
TOTAL UTILITIES	$ _____	per month

For an approximate monthly phone bill, call the phone company to get the basic rates. Don't forget to budget for long distance calls.

Telephone	$ _____	per month

If you expect to have cable TV or special television, determine the cost by calling the local television company.

Cable TV	$ _____	per month

In 1985 average monthly utility bills in four cities[5] were approximately as shown here.*

Los Angeles	$ 82
Houston	$ 87
New York	$151
Kansas City	$ 98

To find your total housing costs, add the items listed below.

MONTHLY RENT OR HOMEOWNER'S EXPENSES

Total monthly cost of residence (house or rental)	$ _____
Total utilities	$ _____
Phone	$ _____
Cable TV	$ _____
TOTAL HOUSING COSTS	$ _____ [1]

Enter at (1) in "Your Monthly Budget" on page 79.

*We have included average figures at times in this budget exercise to give you a starting point for your estimates. The averages are approximate and are not meant to be used as totally accurate portrayals of today's costs. The amounts involved in budgeting make finding your true costs extremely difficult without taking particular circumstances into account. Utilities, for example, vary according to geographical location, type and size of house, amount of insulation, number of residents, etc. In addition, rising prices may make our estimates too low by the time you read them.

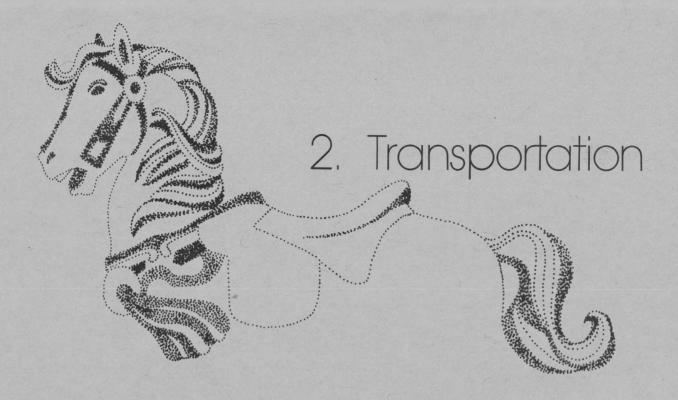

2. Transportation

A few cities offer adequate public transportation, but most people want a car. Whether it's a shiny new sports car or an old jalopy, paying for it and keeping it running will take a sizeable portion of your monthly income.

Describe a car you would like to have when you are 28 years old, or place an ad here for a new or used car.

Let's assume that you have found a car that should serve you well. Let's also assume you don't have enough money to pay the full price in cash, but you do have enough for a down payment. After making a down payment you could get a loan to help pay for the car. Then you would have to make a series of monthly payments. So the next big question is: Can you afford the monthly payments on top of the day to day costs of owning a car? In the table which follows, find the amount closest to the price for the car you chose, and write the monthly payment in the space below the table.

If you finance for 48 months (48 payments):

Loan Amount	Monthly payments		
	16% annual interest	12% annual interest	8% annual interest
$3,000	$ 85	$ 79	$ 73
$5,000	$141	$131	$122
$7,000	$198	$184	$171
$9,000	$255	$237	$220

Monthly payment $ _____

Can you afford monthly payments in addition to the cost of running the car you chose? You will need to buy gasoline. The approximate monthly cost of gasoline can be found by the following procedure.

Estimate the number of miles you might drive per week. Consider:
— Back and forth to work.
— Trips to children's school or daycare center.
— Trips to the store.
— Visits.
— Weekend driving.

EXAMPLE
If Jane drives a small Honda she might get 30 miles to the gallon around town. Her work place is 5 miles from her home, so she drives at least 10 miles a day (5 days a week). Dropping kids off at the babysitter takes another 4 miles a day round trip (5 days a week). Shopping and errands account for another 30 miles a week. On the weekends she averages about 60 miles. Her total mileage is around 150 miles per week. At 30 miles to the gallon Jane needs:

150 ÷ 30 = 5 gallons of gas per week,
or 5 gallons multiplied by the price per gallon.

EXAMPLE
$ .89 per gallon equals
$ .89
x 5
$4.45 per week
x 4   weeks equals $17.80 per month.

Now repeat the calculations with your figures.

Your estimated number of miles per week: _____

Determine the number of miles your car will go on one gallon of gasoline (car dealers or people you know have that information). Remember that estimates in car ads are usually much higher than you will actually get.

Estimated miles per gallon (mpg) _____

Divide the number of miles driven per week by the mpg.

Multiply the number of gallons per week you use by the current price of gasoline per gallon. This will give you the cost of gasoline for a week. To find monthly costs, multiply the weekly cost by four.

Gasoline cost per month $ _____

Every car needs tune-ups, oil and filter changes, and a certain amount of regular maintenance. Tires wear out, and the life of a battery is about three to five years. All these things add to the cost of driving a car. Such costs vary with the size and the complexity of the car. Nevertheless, you can get a rough average by knowing how many cylinders a car's engine has. Choose the monthly average for your car from the list that follows.

Engine cylinders	4	6	8
Average maintenance cost per month	$18	$24	$30

Monthly car maintenance $ _____

Yearly car expenses also include registration or license plate renewal and insurance. Some states only charge a registration fee each year, but others, such as California, include a property tax in the annual license fee. Where this is the case, renewal will be costly for an expensive car, but quite cheap for an old car. If your car is financed, the loan company will require you to have insurance to pay for the car if it is damaged or stolen. If you own your car outright, you can reduce insurance costs by not buying collision insurance. If you make this choice, however, you'll get no help in repairing your car if you have an accident. As you can see, license and insurance costs vary, so your best bet is to ask locally to find out what they would be. If it's any consolation, insurance costs for drivers under age 30 are considerably less for females than for males. (Women have fewer accidents.)

After you have learned the license and insurance costs per year, add them together and divide the total by 12 months to get the cost per month.

Yearly costs:

Car license $ _____

Insurance $ _____

Total yearly costs: $ _____

Costs per month (divide by 12): $ _____

As an alternative to owning a car, public transportation may be available to you. Multiply the cost of one bus, subway, or train ride by the expected number of rides in one month.

Public transportation cost
per month: $ _____

To find your total transportation costs,
add the following items.

Monthly car payments $ _____

Gasoline $ _____

Car maintenance $ _____

License and insurance $ _____

Public transportation $ _____

TOTAL TRANSPORTATION COSTS $ _____ [2]

Enter at (2) in "Your Monthly Budget" on page 79.

3. Clothing

You're probably already familiar with the cost of clothes — at least for yourself. At age 28, however, your wardrobe will have to suit your job. If your work demands it, you may need to buy suits instead of blue jeans and dress shoes instead of tennis shoes. And, if you choose to have children, they will need clothes too. Assume, for the purpose of this exercise, that you already have a basic wardrobe; you only need to replace items or purchase new clothes that you want.

To find your monthly clothing costs, first determine the number of purchases you are likely to make in a year for each clothing category.

For example, how many new dresses do you think you will buy in a year?

Number of dresses _____

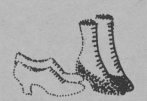

Multiply the number of dresses you will purchase in a year by the average cost of a dress. Do the same for the other items listed below. Then add your totals to get your grand total for a year.

	Number of Purchases	x	Average Cost		TOTAL
Dresses	_____	X	$ _____	= $ _____
Skirts	_____	X	$ _____	= $ _____
Tops	_____	X	$ _____	= $ _____
Pants	_____	X	$ _____	= $ _____
Coats	_____	X	$ _____	= $ _____
Bathing suit	_____	X	$ _____	= $ _____
Pajamas	_____	X	$ _____	= $ _____
Underwear	_____	X	$ _____	= $ _____
Shoes	_____	X	$ _____	= $ _____
Miscellaneous	_____	X	$ _____	= $ _____

GRAND TOTAL
for a year $ _____

Divide the grand total by twelve to learn the monthly average for your clothing expenses.

Grand total of $ _____ divided by 12 equals:

TOTAL COST PER MONTH $ _____

Children

If you expect to have children, figure the cost of clothing for each child. Be sure to consider their ages and the fact that they will not have much they can use from the previous year.

BOY	Number of Purchases	x	Average Cost		TOTAL
Pants	_____	x $ _____		= $	_____
Shirts	_____	x $ _____		= $	_____
Shoes	_____	x $ _____		= $	_____
Underwear	_____	x $ _____		= $	_____
Socks	_____	x $ _____		= $	_____
Jackets	_____	x $ _____		= $	_____
Shorts	_____	x $ _____		= $	_____
Bathing suit	_____	x $ _____		= $	_____
Miscellaneous	_____	x $ _____		= $	_____
			GRAND TOTAL		$ _____

Grand total $ _____ divided by 12 equals

TOTAL COST PER MONTH $ _____

GIRL	Number of Purchases	x	Average Cost		TOTAL
Dresses	_____	x	$ _____	=	$ _____
Pants	_____	x	$ _____	=	$ _____
Tops	_____	x	$ _____	=	$ _____
Coats, jackets	_____	x	$ _____	=	$ _____
Shoes, boots	_____	x	$ _____	=	$ _____
Bathing suit	_____	x	$ _____	=	$ _____
Pajamas	_____	x	$ _____	=	$ _____
Underwear	_____	x	$ _____	=	$ _____
Miscellaneous	_____	x	$ _____	=	$ _____
			GRAND TOTAL		$ _____

Grand total $ _____ divided by 12 equals

TOTAL COST PER MONTH $ _____

Add up all the monthly figures for you and your children to find your total clothing costs.

Your clothing $ _____

Child $ _____

Child $ _____

TOTAL CLOTHING COSTS PER MONTH $ _____ [3]

Enter at (3) in "Your Monthly Budget" on page 79.

4. Food

While it may be possible for a single person to live on yogurt and diet soda, feeding a family takes better planning — and more money. If you've been grocery shopping recently, you already know that. You can use the amount that your family spends on food each week to estimate the cost of feeding your future family. When you make your estimate, remember to include non-food items usually bought at the grocery store. Things like detergent, paper goods, cosmetics, vitamins, and notions add greatly to the average "food" bill.

Estimate your weekly cost and multiply the total by 4 to reach a monthly figure.

Food bill per week $ _____

Multiply by 4   _____ x 4

Monthly cost $ _____

**TOTAL FOOD COSTS
PER MONTH** $ _____ [4]

Enter at (4) in "Your Monthly Budget" on page 79.

The table you see here shows some average food costs for a woman and two children in April 1986. The figures reflect only the cost of food items. The cost of food items is approximately 80 percent of the total grocery store bill. Again, keep in mind that these amounts are only approximate and subject to much variation.

SAMPLE FOOD COSTS[6]

	Thrifty	Low	Moderate	Liberal
Per week	$ 37	$ 46	$ 57	$ 70
Per month	$149	$186	$227	$280

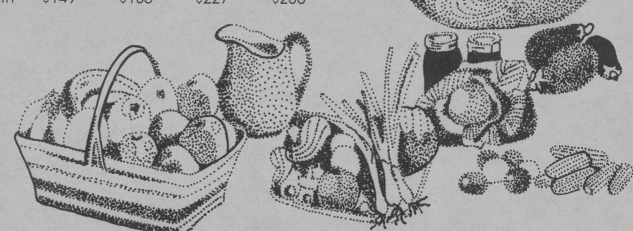

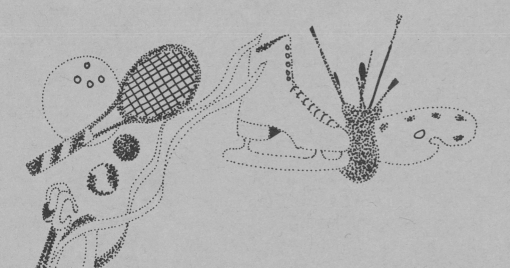

5. Entertainment

Life would be dull if you could only spend money on things that are absolutely necessary. What do you do for fun? Parties? Movies? Skating? What kinds of opportunities do you want to provide for your children? Do you want them to have dance or music lessons, horseback-riding lessons, to be a Scout, or participate in sports?

Hobbies can be expensive. Do you like to go bowling, skating, or to participate in similar activities? Will you want a membership in an athletic club, golf, swim or tennis club? What about buying and maintaining a boat, a hang glider or a horse?

If you would like to take a vacation, you will probably need to save for it. Let's say you want to rent a cabin which costs $360 per week. If so, you would need to save $30 a month for a year to afford one week's rental.

Describe how you imagine you will spend your entertainment dollar when you are 28 years old.

Movies, concerts, etc.	$ _____	per month
Restaurants	$ _____	per month
Children's entertainment and memberships	$ _____	per month
Vacation	$ _____	per month
Hobbies	$ _____	per month
Other entertainment	$ _____	per month
TOTAL ENTERTAINMENT COSTS	$ _____ [5]	per month

Enter at (5) in "Your Monthly Budget" on page 79.

6. Furnishings

You will probably need to buy some items for your apartment, house, or yard. Assume for this exercise that you already have some basic furniture and furnishings. In your estimate, include only additional purchases, such as linens, plants, and decorations. This budget category should also carry some emergency funds to cover unexpected repairs. You'll be glad you set the money aside when the refrigerator fails or you need to replace a hot water heater.

TOTAL FURNISHING COSTS PER MONTH $ _____ [6]

Enter at (6) in "Your Monthly Budget" on page 79.

7. Health Care

Most health care costs are paid by employers as benefits, or "extras" above and beyond wages. However, there are still things left you'll have to pay for yourself.

To figure this cost, assume an employer pays your health insurance, but you pay pharmacy expenses and all doctor's bills less than $100.

Also include in this section the costs of dental bills, glasses, braces, and some drug store articles.

Average health care costs for a family of three might be around $110 per month.

TOTAL HEALTH CARE PER MONTH $ _____ [7]

Enter at (7) in "Your Monthly Budget" on page 79.

Remember to include saving for major, unexpected health problems in your savings section (section nine, upcoming). You can never tell when you or your child will have an acute case of appendicitis, fall off a bike and break an arm, or suffer from a chronic illness.

8. Child Care

If you work and have a child, your child will probably need child care. For example, a five-year-old would need care before or after half-day kindergarten. You will also need to estimate the cost of babysitters for times when you would like to go out alone. Such times should be added to your total child care costs.

To make your estimate, you can check with local daycare facilities to get sample costs, or figure from the hourly rate charged for babysitting.

Total number of hours of care per week	_____
Multiplied by cost per hour	$ _____
Equals cost per week	$ _____

To find the cost per month, multiply the cost per week by four.   x 4

TOTAL CHILD CARE COSTS PER MONTH $ _____ [8]

Enter at (8) in "Your Monthly Budget" on page 79.

9. Savings

How would you like to have a new stereo or take a trip? To buy special things you will probably need to save some money from your paycheck. You also need to think about, and be prepared for, unexpected expenses, like medical bills or a leaky roof. Do you want to send your kids to college? What about retirement? Select a reasonable amount to save each month and write it below.

TOTAL SAVINGS COSTS
PER MONTH $ _____ [9]

Enter at (9) in "Your Monthly Budget" on page 79.

10. Miscellaneous

Toys $ _____ per month

Gifts $ _____ per month

Pets $ _____ per month

Anything else $ _____ per month

TOTAL MISCELLANEOUS COSTS
PER MONTH $ _____ [10]

Enter at (10) in "Your Monthly Budget" on page 79.

Sample Budget

A reasonable budget for a woman with two children living in Dallas, Texas during 1987 might look something like the following.

MONTHLY BUDGET

Housing		
Buying	$ 650	
Renting		$ 350
Transportation	$ 220	
Clothing	$ 115	
Food	$ 280	
Entertainment	$ 50	
Furnishings	$ 50	
Health care	$ 110	
Child care	$ 200	
Savings	$ 50	
Miscellaneous	$ 25	
TOTAL	$1750	$1450

Your Monthly Budget

To determine your total monthly expenses, use the lines you see here to record the amount you arrived at for each preceding numbered section. Adding up all these figures will give you the total amount you can expect to spend in a month, according to your budget.

MONTHLY BUDGET

Housing	(1)	$ _____
Transportation	(2)	$ _____
Clothing	(3)	$ _____
Food	(4)	$ _____
Entertainment	(5)	$ _____
Furnishings	(6)	$ _____
Health care	(7)	$ _____
Child care	(8)	$ _____
Savings	(9)	$ _____
Miscellaneous	(10)	$ _____
TOTAL		$ _____

One More Step

Now that you know how much money it will cost you to live each month, you can go to the want ads and find a job offering that salary, right? Well, not quite. To have enough money to spend, you will need to earn more than the amount you came up with for your budget. The salary offered when you apply for a job, called *gross pay*, is not the amount of money you will take home. The *gross pay* is the salary before taxes and other assessments are subtracted. Money will be withheld (taken out) for Social Security, and state and federal income taxes. Additional amounts for pensions, benefits, or contributions may also be withheld.

Let's assume in this exercise that an average percentage for withholding is 20 percent. This means that if your gross pay is $1,600 a month, you will only take home $1,280. This take-home pay or *net pay* is the money you will be able to spend. The amount you found you would need when you completed your budget should be equal to, or less than, the *net pay* you will take home.

To find the salary you will need to cover the expenses as determined in your budget, divide your monthly net pay by 80 percent.

80% of Gross Pay = Net Pay

Gross Pay = Net Pay divided by .80

EXAMPLE
If your monthly expenses were $1,000 then you would need to earn $1,250 per month in gross pay.

$$X = \text{Gross Pay}$$
$$\text{Net Pay} = \$1,000$$
$$80\% \text{ of } X = \$1,000$$
$$X = 1,000 \text{ divided by } .80$$
$$X = \$1,250$$

To find the yearly net salary you will need, multiply your monthly net salary by 12. You can figure the yearly gross salary needed by substituting the monthly gross salary for the monthly net salary, and multiplying by twelve months.

CONVERTING HOURLY SALARIES TO YEARLY SALARIES

There are 52 weeks per year and the average full-time job is 40 hours per week.

52 weeks a year x 40 hours per week = 2,080 hours per year

2,080 hours per year x $_____ salary per hour = $_____ salary for one year

EXAMPLES
2,080 hours/year x $ 4/hour = $ 8,320/year
2,080 hours/year x $ 5/hour = $10,400/year
2,080 hours/year x $ 6/hour = $12,480/year
2,080 hours/year x $10/hour = $20,800/year
2,080 hours/year x $15/hour = $31,200/year
2,080 hours/year x $20/hour = $41,600/year

Looking for Work

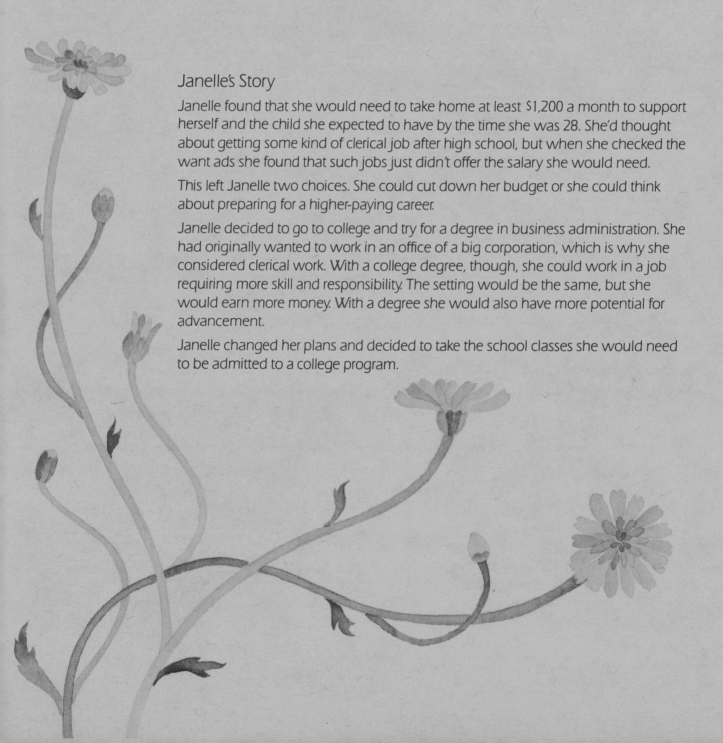

That's it. You've finally arrived at the minimum salary you'll need to earn to support your family in the way you'd like. Now you need to find a job that will pay you that salary. Here are some examples of what other young women found when they completed the budget exercise.

Janelle's Story

Janelle found that she would need to take home at least $1,200 a month to support herself and the child she expected to have by the time she was 28. She'd thought about getting some kind of clerical job after high school, but when she checked the want ads she found that such jobs just didn't offer the salary she would need.

This left Janelle two choices. She could cut down her budget or she could think about preparing for a higher-paying career.

Janelle decided to go to college and try for a degree in business administration. She had originally wanted to work in an office of a big corporation, which is why she considered clerical work. With a college degree, though, she could work in a job requiring more skill and responsibility. The setting would be the same, but she would earn more money. With a degree she would also have more potential for advancement.

Janelle changed her plans and decided to take the school classes she would need to be admitted to a college program.

Susan's Story

After Susan completed her future budget she was amazed to find that she would need nearly $1,400 per month to live and support the two children she wanted to have by age 28. After the death of her father, Susan had watched her mother struggle to pay the monthly bills. To do it, her mother had to work many hours of overtime at the local shop where she clerked.

Susan had originally thought she would be a dental assistant. But when she researched how much it paid, she changed her plans and decided to become a dental technician instead. Although it meant more sacrifice now, (more studying, less partying), and more years in school, Susan knew from her mother's experience that the ability to support a family was necessary for her peace of mind.

Cheryl's Story

Cheryl's mother always said, "You need to have a career you can fall back on in case you're ever a widow and have to support a family." Her mother's message hit home and Cheryl always knew that she wanted that type of insurance.

Cheryl graduated from college with a degree in computer science and then completed her internship with an international computer company. Two years later, Cheryl married. Shortly thereafter she started a family. Cheryl's husband had a good job with an investment firm, so Cheryl changed to minimal part time at work and spent most of her time being a mother.

When the children were five and two years old, Cheryl's husband started drinking. Before long, he was drinking himself into a drunken stupor by early evening—every evening. Cheryl, the relatives, her husband's business associates and the family doctor tried everything they could to get him to stop. Life at home was becoming unbearable. One evening Cheryl returned home after visiting a sick relative in the hospital, to find her husband raging drunkenly and yelling about how the children wouldn't stop crying. She found the baby screaming in her crib with welts obviously inflicted by a belt. Her five-year-old was hiding in the closet, bruised and afraid to come out.

Cheryl picked up the children, walked out of the house, and within a week had an apartment, an attorney and a full time job that would support her family. Cheryl's earlier career planning gave her the option of making the best decisions for her children and allowed her to be a strong and protective mother.

Now Find a Job

As you can see from the preceding example, it pays to think about your future.

What kind of work will you be qualified to do? For information on jobs, how much they pay, and what kinds of skills they require, you might consult:

1. The classified advertising section of your local newspaper.
2. The classified advertising section of a major newspaper from the nearest city of over 500,000 people.
3. The *Occupational Outlook Handbook*, written by the U.S. Department of Labor, which is available in libraries. (A list of sample jobs and job salaries from the *Occupational Outlook Handbook* is included on the following page.)
4. A Career Center, if one is available.

Select a job you think you will qualify for when you are 28 and write the job title and salary in the space provided.

Title _____ Salary _____

Will this job enable you to live the way you want?

To qualify for the job you have chosen, how should you prepare?

Cut out three or four employment ads from the classified section and paste them below.

SAMPLE LIST OF JOBS AND SALARIES*

Architect	$29,000 (1984)	Principal	
Artist (Graphic)	$19,000 (1984)	(Senior High)	$42,000 (1984-85)
Automobile Body		(Junior High)	$40,000 (1984-85)
Repairer	$29,000 (1984)	(Elementary)	$37,000 (1984-85)
Automobile Mechanic	$26,000 (1984)	Psychologist (Ph.D.)	$36,000 (1983)
Bank Teller	$11,000 (1984)	Receptionist	$14,000 (1985)
Bus Driver (Inter City)	$24,000 (1984)	Recreation Worker	$19,000 (1984)
Buyer	$20,000 (1984)	Sales Clerk (Retail)	$15,000 (1984)
Cashier (Union)	$23,000 (1984)	Securities Sales Worker	$64,000 (1984)
Chemist	$34,000 (1984)	School Counselor	$28,000 (1984-85)
Computer Programmer	$26,000 (1984)	Social Worker(MSW)	$26,000 (1984)
Computer Service Technician	$25,000 (1984)	Sociologist	$32,000 (1983)
Cosmetologist	$17,000 (1984)	Teacher	
Dancer	Usually paid by performance. Work is often irregular.	Secondary	$24,000 (1984-1985)
		Elementary	$23,000 (1984-1985)
		Telephone Operator	$15,000 (1984)
Dental Assistant	$12,000 (1984)	Tool and Die Maker	$23,000 (1984)
Designer	$22,000 (1984)	Typist	$15,000 (1984)
Dietician	$28,000 (1984)	Welder	$27,000 (1984)
Economist	$29,000 (1984)		
Electrician	$23,000 (1984)		
Engineer	$41,000 (1985)		
Flight Attendant	$23,000 (1984)		
Forester	$31,000 (1984)		
Hotel Manager	$30,000 (1983)		
Lawyer	$88,000 (1984)		
Legal Assistant	$20,000 (1984)		
Mail Carrier	$25,000 (1985)		
Nurse	$21,000 (1984)		
Photographer	$24,000 (1984)		
Physician	$108,000 (1984)		
Physical Therapist	$25,000 (1985)		
Pilot	$80,000 (1984)		
Plumber	$21,000 (1984)		
Police Officer (Patrol)	$21,000 (1984)		

*All figures are given to the nearest thousand. The amounts shown are averages. These figures are average figures subject to many variations in individual circumstances. In some cases, annual figures have been computed from hourly wages, based on a 40 hour work week for a full year. Actual work hours may differ, causing inaccuracies in the annual salaries listed.

REFLECTIONS

CHAPTER FOUR

Knowing What You Want Out of Life

Values and goal setting

Whenever two good people argue
over principles, they are both right.
— Marie Ebner von Eschenbach
    Austrian Author

You have to know exactly what you
want out of your career. If you want
to be a star, you don't bother with
other things.
— Marilyn Horne
    Opera Singer

Your Values

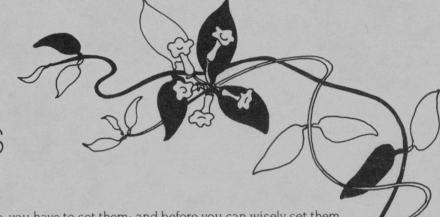

Before you can achieve any goals in life, you have to set them; and before you can wisely set them, you need to decide what is most important to you, and just how important it is.

Some of your possessions are more important than others. Some of your activities are more enjoyable, or more meaningful than others. If you were to state your goals for the future, some things would be at the top of the list and others far below. We use the term "values" to refer to all of the preceding, and more. Your personal values may place extra importance on possessions, religion, friendship, marriage, work, or any number of other things. Until you have a clear sense of what's important to you — your values — it will be difficult to make informed decisions about your future.

cathy   **by Cathy Guisewite**

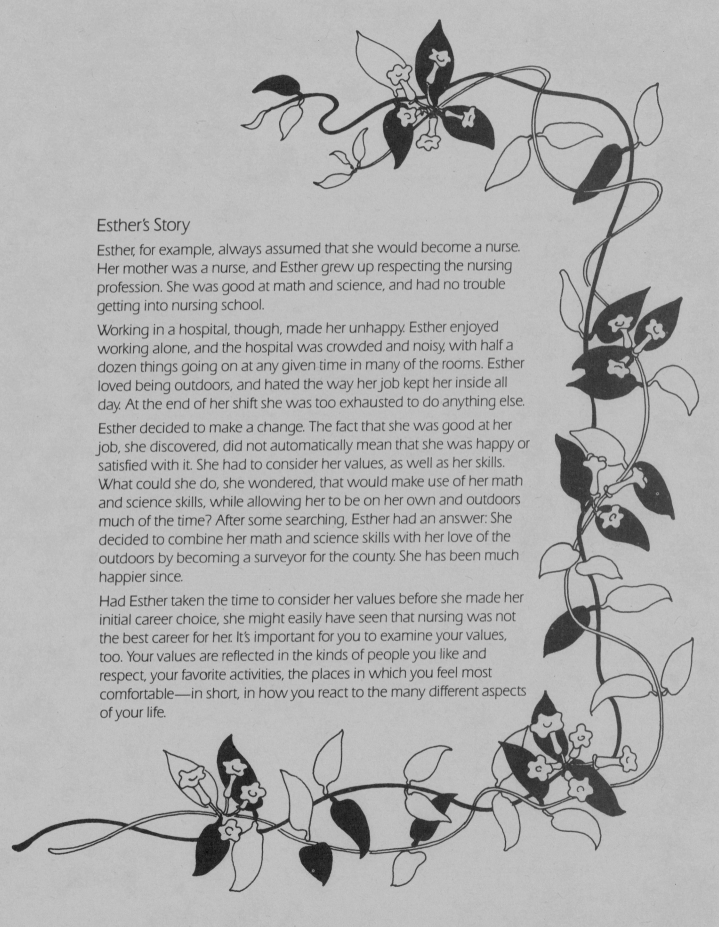

Esther's Story

Esther, for example, always assumed that she would become a nurse. Her mother was a nurse, and Esther grew up respecting the nursing profession. She was good at math and science, and had no trouble getting into nursing school.

Working in a hospital, though, made her unhappy. Esther enjoyed working alone, and the hospital was crowded and noisy, with half a dozen things going on at any given time in many of the rooms. Esther loved being outdoors, and hated the way her job kept her inside all day. At the end of her shift she was too exhausted to do anything else.

Esther decided to make a change. The fact that she was good at her job, she discovered, did not automatically mean that she was happy or satisfied with it. She had to consider her values, as well as her skills. What could she do, she wondered, that would make use of her math and science skills, while allowing her to be on her own and outdoors much of the time? After some searching, Esther had an answer: She decided to combine her math and science skills with her love of the outdoors by becoming a surveyor for the county. She has been much happier since.

Had Esther taken the time to consider her values before she made her initial career choice, she might easily have seen that nursing was not the best career for her. It's important for you to examine your values, too. Your values are reflected in the kinds of people you like and respect, your favorite activities, the places in which you feel most comfortable—in short, in how you react to the many different aspects of your life.

There are no right or wrong values when it comes to making a decision about a future career. You just need to be sure that they are *yours*, not those of your best friend, or the star of your favorite TV show.

The exercise that follows will help you determine what your values are right now. By taking a look at what you like to do, and why you like to do it, you may begin to learn some of the values that should play a part in your career choice.

WHAT DO I ENJOY DOING?[7]

List 20 things you like to do, such as bike riding, going to parties, studying, playing tennis, writing, and so forth. Use the spaces provided under the word "Activities."

ACTIVITIES	1	2	3	4	5	6	7	8	9
1.									
2.									
3.									
4.									
5.									
6.									
7.									
8.									
9.									
10.									
11.									
12.									
13.									
14.									
15.									
16.									
17.									
18.									
19.									
20.									

To the right of each activity:

In column 1:   write a **P** if the activity is usually done with people. Write an **A** if it is usually done alone.

In column 2:   write a **$** if the activity costs more than $5.

In column 3:   write an **O** if the activity is usually done outdoors. Write an **I** if it is usually done indoors.

In column 4:   write an **M** if your mother would probably have the activity on her list.

In column 5:   write an **H** if it is very important that a future husband include this activity on his list.

In column 6:   write an **O** if you now do this activity often, an **ST** if you do it sometimes, and an **R** if it is done rarely.

In column 7:   write a **2** if you would have listed the activity two years ago.

In column 8:   write an **A** if the activity requires you to be active physically. write a **P** if the activity is physically passive.

In column 9:   rank the **5** activities you like best, in the order of importance from **1** to **5** (1 = most important; 5 = least important).

Now examine the table to see if any themes or patterns are apparent in what you like to do. Is there a pattern in the underlying values too?

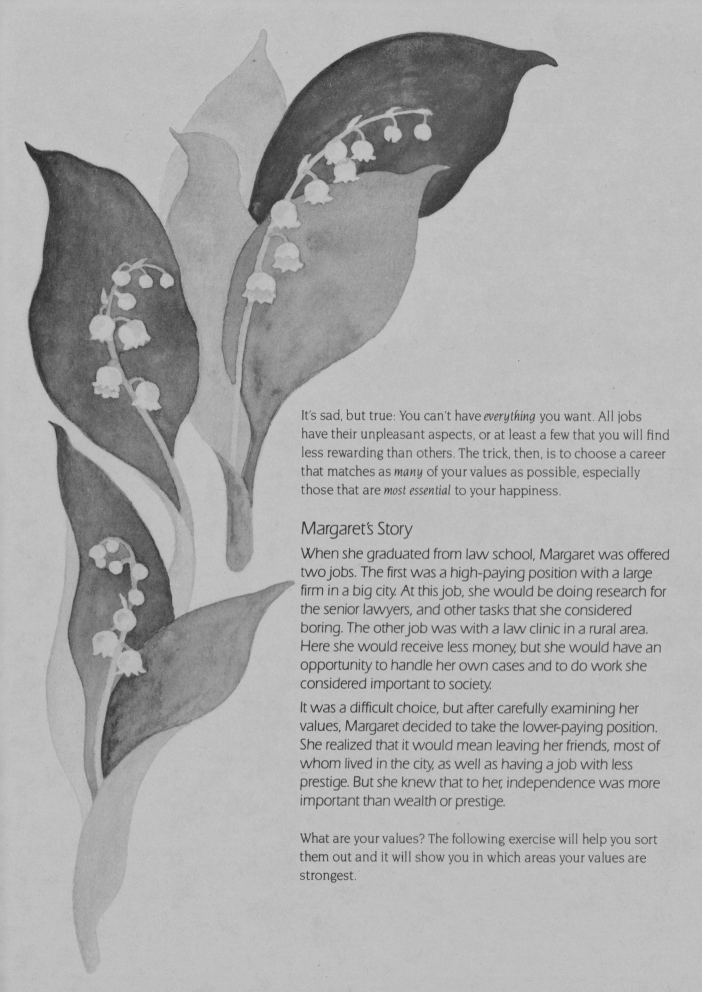

It's sad, but true: You can't have *everything* you want. All jobs have their unpleasant aspects, or at least a few that you will find less rewarding than others. The trick, then, is to choose a career that matches as *many* of your values as possible, especially those that are *most essential* to your happiness.

Margaret's Story

When she graduated from law school, Margaret was offered two jobs. The first was a high-paying position with a large firm in a big city. At this job, she would be doing research for the senior lawyers, and other tasks that she considered boring. The other job was with a law clinic in a rural area. Here she would receive less money, but she would have an opportunity to handle her own cases and to do work she considered important to society.

It was a difficult choice, but after carefully examining her values, Margaret decided to take the lower-paying position. She realized that it would mean leaving her friends, most of whom lived in the city, as well as having a job with less prestige. But she knew that to her, independence was more important than wealth or prestige.

What are your values? The following exercise will help you sort them out and it will show you in which areas your values are strongest.

VALUES SURVEY

Check the column that most closely matches your feelings.

		Very True	Some-times True	Not Sure	Not True
1.	I would rather have a large expensive house than own a work of art.				
2.	I like to go places with my friends.				
3.	I'd really like to travel to far away places.				
4.	I think music and art should be required in our schools.				
5.	It is important that my family does things together.				
6.	I like to make things.				
7.	I would rather be president of a club than just a member.				
8.	I'd like people to know that I've done something well.				
9.	I like to read books that help me understand people.				
10.	If I had talent, I'd like to be on TV.				
11.	Having an expensive car is something I'd really like.				
12.	If I could, I'd like to make a movie that would make people aware of injustice, and would improve the conditions it described.				
13.	I'd rather be rich than married.				
14.	I like writing stories, plays, or poetry.				
15.	I like to try things I've never done before.				
16.	I enjoy doing different things.				
17.	It is important to be proud of what I do.				
18.	If my friends want to do something that I think is wrong, I will not do it.				
19.	I'd like to accomplish something in life that will be well known.				
20.	A strong family unit is essential to me.				
21.	I would disobey a boss who asked me to do something against my principles, even if it meant being fired.				
22.	It is important for me to have a good understanding of history.				
23.	If I could, I'd like to be president.				
24.	It would be fun to climb mountains.				
25.	It is very important for me to live in beautiful surroundings.				
26.	I like to go to parties.				
27.	It is important to have very good friends.				

	Very True	Some-times True	Not Sure	Not True
28. I would rather make gifts than buy them.				
29. I am very close to my mother, father, or both.				
30. I like to attend lectures from which I can learn something.				
31. It is more important to stick to my beliefs than to make money.				
32. I would rather make less money at a job I know would last than take a chance with a job that might not last but pays more.				
33. I would like a lot of expensive possessions.				
34. I would rather be free to move around than be tied down by a family.				
35. I like to feel that I am in charge in a group.				
36. It is important to have an appreciation for art or music.				
37. I like to write.				
38. I'd look forward to taking a job in a city I had never visited before.				
39. Having children is important to me.				
40. I'd like to understand the way a TV works.				
41. I'd like to be able to decide what and how much work I will do during a day.				
42. I'd like to do something that helps people.				
43. I'd like to be famous.				
44. I'd rather be a judge than a lawyer.				
45. I do not think I'd like adventurous vacations.				
46. I would like to have works of art in my home.				
47. I would like a job that gives me plenty of free time to spend with my family.				
48. I could not be happy with a job in which I did not feel good about myself.				
49. I get very nervous when I'm forced to take chances.				
50. I would rather be a boss than a worker.				
51. It is important to share activities with friends.				
52. If I knew how, I would make my own clothes.				
53. I would rather not have to answer to a boss.				

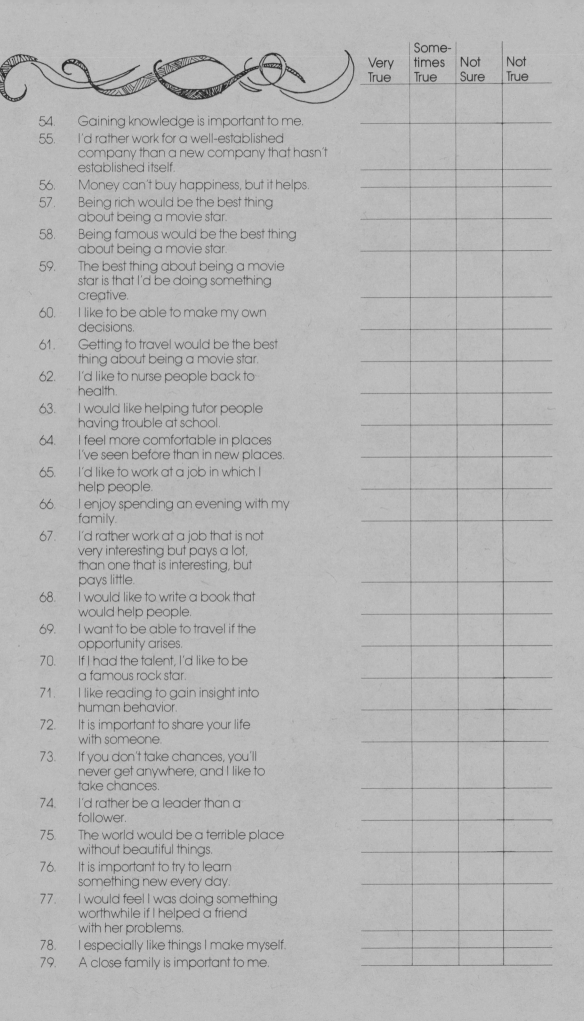

	Very True	Some-times True	Not Sure	Not True
54. Gaining knowledge is important to me.				
55. I'd rather work for a well-established company than a new company that hasn't established itself.				
56. Money can't buy happiness, but it helps.				
57. Being rich would be the best thing about being a movie star.				
58. Being famous would be the best thing about being a movie star.				
59. The best thing about being a movie star is that I'd be doing something creative.				
60. I like to be able to make my own decisions.				
61. Getting to travel would be the best thing about being a movie star.				
62. I'd like to nurse people back to health.				
63. I would like helping tutor people having trouble at school.				
64. I feel more comfortable in places I've seen before than in new places.				
65. I'd like to work at a job in which I help people.				
66. I enjoy spending an evening with my family.				
67. I'd rather work at a job that is not very interesting but pays a lot, than one that is interesting, but pays little.				
68. I would like to write a book that would help people.				
69. I want to be able to travel if the opportunity arises.				
70. If I had the talent, I'd like to be a famous rock star.				
71. I like reading to gain insight into human behavior.				
72. It is important to share your life with someone.				
73. If you don't take chances, you'll never get anywhere, and I like to take chances.				
74. I'd rather be a leader than a follower.				
75. The world would be a terrible place without beautiful things.				
76. It is important to try to learn something new every day.				
77. I would feel I was doing something worthwhile if I helped a friend with her problems.				
78. I especially like things I make myself.				
79. A close family is important to me.				

	Very True	Some-times True	Not Sure	Not True
80. I think it is important to donate to the needy.				
81. I enjoy looking at beautiful scenery.				
82. The best thing about winning a gold medal at the Olympics would be the recognition.				
83. I like to go on hikes (or bike rides) with my friends.				
84. I have strong beliefs about what is right and wrong.				
85. It is important to have a family with whom to discuss problems.				
86. I'd like an exciting life.				
87. I prefer working by myself rather than as part of a team.				
88. I'd like to know all that I can about the workings of nature.				
89. I think it's wrong to help a friend cheat on an exam, even if I know he will fail if I don't help.				
90. Having a job I know I can keep is important to me.				
91. I'd like to have enough money to invest for the future.				
92. I don't like someone assigning me tasks to do.				
93. I do not like being alone very much.				
94. I like to take charge of organizing activities.				
95. I think saving money for the future is very important.				
96. When I've done something I'm proud of, it's important that other people know.				
97. I would rather make less money at a job in which I choose my own work, than make more money at a job in which someone tells me what to do.				
98. People should contribute a small amount of money to be used to decorate public buildings.				
99. I don't like to take risks with money.				
100. I like thinking of something that's never been done before.				
101. I would not like a job in which I traveled a lot and could not have lasting relationships.				
102. If a teacher accidentally left test answers where I could see them, I would not look.				
103. I like people to ask me for my opinion when trying to decide the best way to handle a situation.				
104. If I could, I'd like to make a movie that people would think is beautiful.				

Turn back to the first page of this exercise. Above the words "Very True," write a 9. Above the words "Sometimes True," write a 6. Above the words "Not Sure," write a 3. Above the words "Not True," write a 0. Do the same for each page of the exercise.

Now, for each number listed below, write the numerical value of the response you selected. For example, if on number 1 you selected "Sometimes True," put a 6 on the line next to number 1. When all the lines have been completed, total the numerical responses under each heading.

Family	Adventure	Knowledge	Power
5 _____	3 _____	9 _____	7 _____
20 _____	15 _____	22 _____	23 _____
29 _____	16 _____	30 _____	35 _____
39 _____	24 _____	40 _____	44 _____
47 _____	38 _____	54 _____	50 _____
66 _____	61 _____	71 _____	74 _____
79 _____	73 _____	76 _____	94 _____
85 _____	86 _____	88 _____	103 _____
Total _____	Total _____	Total _____	Total _____

Moral Judgment and Personal Consistency	Money or Wealth	Friendship and Companionship	Recognition
17 _____	1 _____	2 _____	8 _____
18 _____	11 _____	26 _____	10 _____
21 _____	13 _____	27 _____	19 _____
31 _____	33 _____	51 _____	43 _____
48 _____	56 _____	72 _____	58 _____
84 _____	57 _____	83 _____	70 _____
89 _____	67 _____	93 _____	82 _____
102 _____	91 _____	101 _____	96 _____
Total _____	Total _____	Total _____	Total _____

Independence and Freedom	Security	Beauty or Aesthetics	Creativity	Helping Others
34 _____	32 _____	4 _____	6 _____	12 _____
41 _____	45 _____	25 _____	14 _____	42 _____
53 _____	49 _____	36 _____	28 _____	62 _____
60 _____	55 _____	46 _____	37 _____	63 _____
69 _____	64 _____	75 _____	52 _____	65 _____
87 _____	90 _____	81 _____	59 _____	68 _____
92 _____	95 _____	98 _____	78 _____	77 _____
97 _____	99 _____	104 _____	100 _____	80 _____
Total _____	Total _____	Total _____	Total _____	Total _____

For which category is your total the highest? That's the value most important to you at present. However, values can change, and in fact, usually do. For this reason, you may wish to take the Values Survey again in a year or two.

What do the categories mean? Descriptions of each category follow.

Family

Someone with a very high score in this category greatly values the closeness of a family. Parents and children feel close to each other and spend much time together. "Family" can also mean other persons or friends who are close to you, if you choose not to join a traditional family. Your inner circle of acquaintances is important. You are a people person. If you score high in this area, you will want a job that allows you plenty of time at home where you can enjoy family and friends. Your work hours should be consistent and stable. You probably would not be happy as a traveling sales representative, a forest ranger, or a nun.

Adventure

In contrast to the preceding, a career that calls for a lot of travel may be just right if you value adventure. You certainly would not be satisfied with a job in which the routine is the same day after day. Your score shows that you would like to have varied job duties and that you are comfortable taking risks.

See how easy this is? But, oops! What if you have high scores in two categories? Could you have a happy family life and lots of adventure, too? It's possible. Here is where you have to make some choices and spend time comparing careers. Which do you value more? If you're an adventure-loving family woman, you may have to settle for hang gliding on weekends, or making an expedition through the wilderness each summer, rather than being a foreign correspondent or an international jewel trader.

Knowledge

If you value knowledge, you will want a career that lets you keep on learning. Teaching is an obvious choice, but you might also consider doing research — scientific, historical, political, or whatever. Being a journalist who covers different stories every day and spends time reading reports and interviewing people might also be a good choice.

Power

It's hard to find an entry-level job with a lot of power, but if that's what you value, you'll want to make sure that there's plenty of room for advancement in your chosen field. You should prepare yourself to take a leadership role by pursuing advanced education or by learning more skills in your field. Or, you might want to start your own business. That way you can be president immediately — even if you're the only employee!

Moral Judgment and Personal Consistency

If you scored high in this category, you'll want to make sure that your career choice is one you feel is worthwhile; that is, one you can be proud of, no matter what other values it mirrors. For example, if you also had a high adventure score, you would probably be more satisfied as a Peace Corps worker than as a bomber pilot.

Money

Obviously, if money is your top value, you will look carefully at potential earnings for any job you take. Since making a lot of money usually entails spending long hours on the job, you should consider your other values in choosing a field which will hold your interest. You may have little time for family, friends, or outside hobbies. Check the salary levels of a wide range of jobs before starting to narrow your choices.

Friendship and Companionship

If friendship and companionship are important to you, your job should involve working closely with others. Being shut away in a laboratory or sitting in a cubicle with an adding machine will probably hold few charms for you. If you get along well with others and can talk easily with people you don't know well, you might consider working in sales or public relations. If having time for close friendships outside of work is important, though, you won't want a job that involves a great deal of travel or overtime.

Recognition

Is recognition what you want? If so, you'll do best choosing something for which you have a talent, something that will let you work to develop the talent. Of course, some fields have more potential for recognition built into them than others. There may be very few world-renowned bus drivers, but the fact remains that in many communities there are bus drivers *everyone* knows and respects. It often depends on how you do your job, not just what job you do.

Aesthetics

People who score high in aesthetics (love of beauty) like to be surrounded by beauty. If this describes you, you might be happy as an interior designer or an art dealer. You might like being a forest ranger at a national park or an executive in a plush office. You would almost certainly be unhappy as a garbage collector or coal miner.

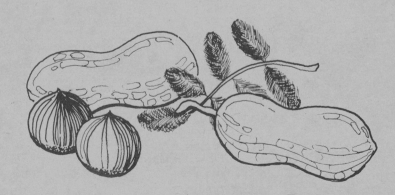

Creativity

Writers and artists are often thought of as creative, but creativity is an important asset in other fields as well. If you value creativity, you will want a career that gives you room to make choices and decisions, to put your ideas into effect, and to evaluate the results of your efforts. You probably wouldn't be happy in a job that is rigid or inflexible. You might find a use for your creativity by working as a program director for a senior citizens' group, as an engineer in a large research firm, or as a landscape architect.

Helping Others

Women who value helping others have traditionally become teachers and nurses. But, there are many other options. Doctors, social workers, psychologists, counselors, writers, politicians, lawyers, dieticians, speech pathologists, and physical therapists are just a few of the career possibilities for those scoring high in this area.

Independence

If you value independence and freedom, you should beware of careers which are rigidly supervised or scheduled. Some sales representative positions allow you a great deal of freedom. People who work on a free-lance basis, or as consultants, may be able to decide where, when, and how much work they will do.

Security

Careers with well-established companies, or those in areas that are basic to human needs and not likely to become obsolete, are good choices for someone who values security. Such a person is usually happier with clearly defined work.

Re-examine your values throughout your life to make sure you aren't working hard and giving up things that are important to you for the sake of something you no longer value.

Here's a quick exercise to help demonstrate how each value relates to career choices. Check the choice that would be most reasonable for a person with the value stated in each question.

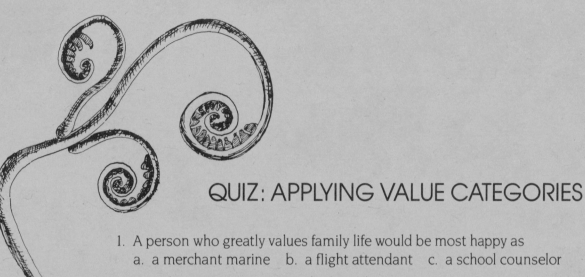

QUIZ: APPLYING VALUE CATEGORIES

1. A person who greatly values family life would be most happy as
   a. a merchant marine   b. a flight attendant   c. a school counselor

2. An adventurous person might consider a career as
   a. an accountant   b. an overseas diplomat   c. a florist

3. Knowledge and continued learning would be most important in
   a. college teaching   b. working on an assembly line   c. typing

4. A person concerned with power would be best advised to seek a college degree in
   a. philosophy   b. business administration   c. English

5. Moral judgment plays an important part in
   a. cosmetology   b. counseling   c. welding

6. Those most concerned with money might want to be
   a. social workers   b. corporation heads   c. playground supervisors

7. Companionship would be an important part of a job as
   a. a phone installer   b. a tour guide   c. a jewelry repair person

8. Recognition would be most likely gained as
   a. an athlete   b. a plumber   c. a mail deliverer

9. Valuing aesthetics would be especially important for
   a. a truck driver   b. a veterinarian   c. an art critic

10. A person with a need for some creativity might be happiest as
    a. waitress   b. a cook   c. a cashier

11. Those who want to help others would get the most satisfaction from
    a. film editing   b. scoring music   c. driving an ambulance

12. A person who values independence should investigate a career as
    a. a secretary   b. a free-lance writer   an accountant

13. Security would be one advantage to a job as
    a. an assembly line worker   b. a model   c. a manager with a well-established company

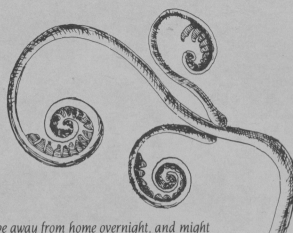

ANSWERS

1. The answer is *c*. A school counselor would seldom have to be away from home overnight, and might even have hours like those of her children in school. She might be able to share summer vacations with them, and so forth.

2. The answer is *b*. Living in various parts of the world would provide many opportunities for adventure.

3. The answer here, of course, is *a*. A college teacher must not only be very knowledgeable, but must keep on learning.

4. *b* is the correct answer. This degree would make you eligible for management or executive jobs with the government or with large and powerful corporations.

5. The correct answer is *b*. Counselors have a great deal of influence over their clients, and must be careful about any suggestions they make.

6. The answer is *b*. American corporation executives are among the most highly paid people in the world.

7. The correct answer is *b*. Getting along well with people is essential for the work of tour guide.

8. The answer is *a*. It's difficult to gain recognition in a field in which there is little media attention or public interest.

9. The correct choice is *c*. An art critic's sensibilities must be very well-developed.

10. The answer is *b*. With the proper training, cooks or chefs can be extremely creative in their work.

11. The correct answer is *c*. Although some solitary professions may also be helpful to others, you probably won't get as much satisfaction from them as you would from working directly with others and seeing the results.

12. The answer is *b*. Keep in mind that jobs offering greater independence than others often entail more risk as well.

13. The answer is *c*. Jobs that depend heavily on factors that may be beyond your control, such as the economy, or your own youth and beauty, are not good choices for you if you are interested in security.

Return to the Values Survey and look at the three categories for which your value scores were highest and write them here.

_____

_____

_____

Now put on your thinking cap and come up with a career or type of work that combines the three values you listed. As you are thinking, be sure to keep your income requirements from the budget section in mind.

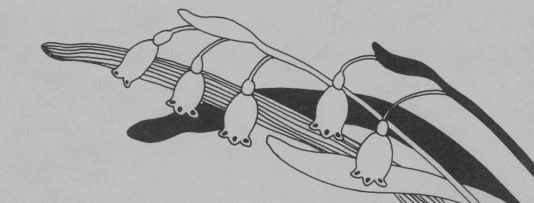

Ginny's Thoughts

Ginny's top three values were power, recognition, and helping others. When she thought about jobs that involve power, she came up with a list that included business executive, judge, fashion designer, and politician. Ginny knew that there were other jobs that fit, but her list was a start.

Recognition was a trickier area. Realistically, she had to admit that she had no great talent as an athlete, singer, or movie star. When she looked back at her "power" list, however, she thought it might be quite possible to make a name for herself in one of those fields.

What about helping others? There were many possibilities, of course. But fields like nursing and social work didn't seem to hold much promise for power and recognition. Looking back at her list, she decided that, while business executives could certainly help society, business was not the right path for her. Fashion designers could be said to be helpful to others, but that really wasn't what she had in mind. Now, judges and politicians . . . "Hmm," she thought, "maybe I should think about going to law school, the place to start for either of those professions."

What about you? Can you come up with some careers that have elements of each of your top three values?

How do your present values relate to careers you might choose? Quickly think of jobs which encompass your values. Get your family or friends to help, and complete the sentences below.

I should look into finding out more about becoming a _____

_____

because I value _____

_____

_____

_____

and this career would allow me to _____

_____

_____

_____

I should look into finding out more about becoming a _____

_____

because I value _____

_____

_____

_____

and this career would allow me to _____

_____

_____

_____

Did you come up with any new careers you'd like to investigate further?

_____

Now that you have looked at the activities you like to do, and more generally, at the things you value, reflect on your conclusions and write a statement about them.

What is Most Important to Me?

_____

_____

_____

_____

_____

_____

_____

_____

_____

_____

_____

_____

_____

_____

_____

_____

_____

_____

Date _____

Goal Setting

Have you ever stopped to wonder what makes some people successful? Talents and abilities are certainly important, but an equally important aspect of success is knowing what you want. When you do, you can consciously choose actions that will lead toward your goal.

Major businesses define what they want and where they are going by setting goals, and then listing ways to achieve those goals. Their plans for meeting the goal are called objectives. Objectives, in other words, are the measurable steps you will take to reach your goal. Successful people often use the same approach to help them plan their actions.

Lynn's Story

Lynn wanted to lose 15 pounds by the beginning of summer vacation. She followed a diet with menus of under 1,000 calories a day, and started a daily exercise program. She weighed herself each morning and kept a progress chart inside her closet door—right next to a picture of the lifeguard she had a crush on. She allowed herself a reasonable amount of time to lose weight. She charted her progress, kept her goal in mind, and she met it!

Lynn looked terrific at the beach in her new bathing suit, and attracted the attention of the lifeguard. Once he opened his mouth, though, she realized that his ego was as big as his biceps, and she had better things to do with her summer. So, she set a new goal—to run in the Labor Day marathon.

By looking back at Lynn's story, you can see the importance of having a goal. Goals identify a desired behavior or achievement to be completed within a set amount of time. After a goal is set, it really helps if you can measure progress toward it. Lynn's first goal could be measured by weighing herself on the first day of summer vacation — either she had lost the 15 pounds or she hadn't. If she finishes the marathon on Labor Day, she will have reached her second goal.

Goals need to be measured so that you can clearly determine whether or not you have achieved them. Setting a completion date or deadline not only tells you whether or not you have been successful, but helps you set up plans for specific actions.

While Lynn was dieting, her first objective was to limit her daily food intake to 1,000 calories. The second was to carry out ten exercises on a daily schedule. She did a bit of research and learned that if she followed this schedule she could be assured a reasonable chance of success. If she is also going to finish the marathon, she will have to set objectives concerning the number of miles she must run each week. That way, she will be in condition by the time of the race.

The more specific you can be in stating a goal and your steps for reaching it, the better your chance for success. General goals such as, "I want to be happy," or "I want to be a success," need to be broken down into smaller, more immediately attainable parts. What would make you happy? Would you consider yourself successful if you were rich? How much money would you need to feel you were rich?

An example of a more specific goal would be, "to make $50,000 a year by the time I'm 30."

With this goal, objectives could be:

1. By age 15, research ten careers that pay $50,000 a year.
2. Take a vocational interest survey by age 15.
3. By age 16, apply to four colleges or training schools that prepare for possible career choices.
4. By age 17, take classes that will meet college entrance requirements.

Another example of a specific goal could be to be married to the same person for life.

Objectives for this goal could be:

1. By age 19, list my values and those I would like my partner to share.
2. Spend one day a week in activities in which I would be likely to meet someone who shares my interests: church, hikes, folk dancing, and music programs, for example.
3. Once married, set aside at least one hour a day for total attention to my partner.

The second example we've described illustrates that with any goal you choose, there's no guarantee that you will be successful. No one can say with certainty that you will marry and stay married for 25 years. However, there are many things you can do to improve your chances for success. You can make sure you understand yourself and that you take part in activities that will increase your chances of meeting someone with whom you are compatible. Later, you can engage in activities that will help enrich and maintain your marriage.

Set Your Own Goals

Direct practice is the most effective method for learning to set and use goals and objectives.

Write four goals that you would like to achieve for each time period listed here. As you write, consider whether or not the goal can be measured. That is, will you be able to tell without a doubt if your goal has been reached?

Today's Goals

EXAMPLE: Finish my paper for English.

1. _____

_____

2. _____

_____

3. _____

_____

4. _____

_____

This Week's Goals

EXAMPLE: Run a total of 20 miles.

1. _____
   _____

2. _____
   _____

3. _____
   _____

4. _____
   _____

This Year's Goals

EXAMPLE: Write for catalogues of five colleges or trade schools I might want to attend.

1. _____
   _____

2. _____
   _____

3. _____
   _____

4. _____
   _____

"By the Time I'm 25" Goals

EXAMPLE: Earn a Master's Degree in Business Administration.

1. _____
   _____

2. _____
   _____

3. _____
   _____

4. _____
   _____

Objectives

The Action Plan

1. What will be different?
2. By how many, or how much?
3. By when?

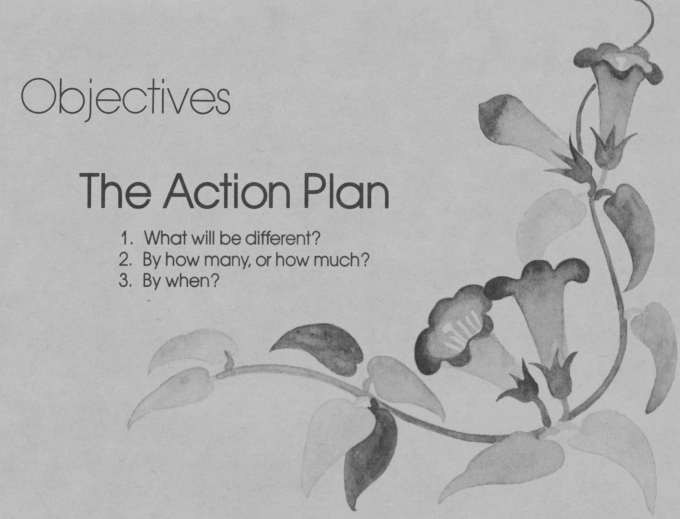

Setting goals is one thing. *Reaching* your goals will require specific actions on your part. But why? How do you know what your objectives should be? It sometimes takes *research* to come up with a sound action plan.

If your goals are very specific, objectives will often suggest themselves. If you want to lose 15 pounds in ten weeks, you will need to lose a pound and a half each week. By research you will find that you need to limit your eating to 1,200 calories a day. When objectives are less obvious, it may help to ask yourself these questions: What will be different when I have reached my goal? By how many, or how much? By when?

Diagramming your objectives can be a big help. Once you learn how, you'll find that stating them becomes almost automatic. Here's how to diagram. Begin by asking yourself, "What will be different?" *Underline* it. Then ask, "By how many?" Use a triangle, like the one in the example that follows, to show this step. "By when?" Draw a circle around the date.

> EXAMPLE
> If your goal is to make your own holiday gifts, an objective might be to knit three pair of mittens by December 15. A diagram of this objective would look like this:
>
> To knit three pair of mittens by December 15.

For practice, diagram the objectives for the goals that follow.

EXERCISE 1: Diagramming Goals and Objectives

Goal: Win a piano competition next April.

Objective: Learn two piano concertos by September.

                         Practice one hour a day, six days a week.

Goal: Buy a car before Christmas.

Objective: Save $50 a month for the next 10 months.

                         Visit two car lots by mid-November.

Goal: Get in shape for a backpacking trip in six weeks.

Objective: Go on a one-day hike each week for the next five weeks.

                         Do 100 leg lifts a day for the next six weeks.

Goal: Get an "A" in history this semester.

Objective: Complete each history assignment by the day it is due.

                         Read all assignments before each class. Study history one

                         hour a night all semester.

Now write and diagram *two objectives* for each of the following goals. Make sure that each of your objectives includes all three of the diagram components.

Goal: Get a part time job this summer.

Objective: _____

Objective: _____

Goal: Increase my typing speed by 20 words a minute.

Objective: _____

Objective: _____

Goal: Get an "A" in my math class this semester.

Objective: _____

Objective: _____

What goals have you set for yourself? To get practice setting objectives, write one goal that you hope to achieve in high school, one goal involving your friends, and one goal for your future. Set two objectives for each goal and diagram them to show what will be different, by how much, and by when.

EXERCISE 2: Writing Goals and Objectives

1. Write one goal with two objectives that involves high school.

Goal: _____

_____

Objective: _____

_____

Objective: _____

_____

2. Write one goal with two objectives that involves friends.

Goal: _____

_____

Objective: _____

_____

Objective: _____

_____

3. Write one goal with two objectives that relates to your future.

Goal: _____

_____

Objective: _____

_____

Objective: _____

_____

4. Write one goal and two objectives that relate to your achieving a behavior you consider desirable for yourself. Turn back to page 31 and review the desired behavior change.

Goal: _____

_____

Objective: _____

_____

Objective: _____

_____

REFLECTIONS

On this narrow planet, we have only the choice between two unknown worlds.
— Colette
  French writer

No trumpets sound when the important decisions of our life are made. Destiny is made known silently.
— Agnes De Mille
  Choreographer

CHAPTER FIVE

How Do You Get There From Here?

Decision making

If you've ever felt controlled by events or by others, you know how upsetting it can be. One of life's worst frustrations is feeling that you have no control over your own actions. In contrast, there are few greater satisfactions than choosing your own direction in life and making things go your own way. How do people gain such control? Most have learned to consciously make decisions that reflect their *values* and *goals*.

Keeping your values and goals in mind when you make decisions is not as hard as it might sound. In fact, you probably already do it in many situations. Remember that sweater your great Aunt Lucy — the one who lives across the country — sent you? The one with all those dingle-balls that made you look as if you were impersonating a kitchen curtain? Because you *valued* her thoughtfulness, you promptly sent a thank you note. And, because your *goal* is to be a person with taste and consideration for others, you quickly made the *decision* to hide the sweater in the back of your sister's closet. (You wouldn't want a burglar or anyone else who might happen to sneak into your closet to think that *you* owned the sweater.)

Choosing a proper course of action is often more difficult than it was with Aunt Lucy's sweater. What are the steps to making better decisions when things are less clear cut? In this chapter you will learn a logical step-by-step way to keep your values and goals in focus. You should find it helpful in almost any situation.

Sandy's Story

For Sandy, every morning seems to start the same way. The alarm clock blares its unwelcome message and Sandy, still half asleep, knocks it to the floor in an attempt to silence it. "I should have gone to bed earlier," she says to herself. But it's too late to think about that now. She decides to stay in bed just a little longer. The ten minutes of stolen sleep leave little time to think about what to wear or what to have for breakfast.

Soon she's charging down the hall at school to her locker. From there she barely makes it to her first-period class before the bell. Today's the day she has to decide what classes to take next year. She tried to think about it before, but it was so hard, and there always seemed to be something better to do.

Sandy thinks, "I guess I'll go to college; my parents want me to." But she really isn't sure. She isn't sure of anything. Then she thinks of Rick. He always seems to know what he wants. But, even though she likes him a lot, she's not sure that what he wants is best for her. Sometimes she thinks she'd like to go out with other guys.

Sandy's parents want her to study. Jody wants her to come to her party. Rick wants her to go to the football game. But what about her? What does she want?

Have you ever felt like Sandy? Have you ever felt as if the world was spinning away from you and you didn't know what to do? Sometimes the constant decisions of daily living make people feel that way. Think about a typical day for a school girl; you, if you like. Write down ten decisions a girl might make during a typical day.

1. _____
2. _____
3. _____
4. _____
5. _____
6. _____
7. _____
8. _____
9. _____
10. _____

Decision Making:
A Lifelong Process

Making decisions starts in infancy and continues throughout our lives. The kinds of decisions we make change as our lives progress. For comparison, list some decisions a person might make at the ages given here.

5 years old _____

_____

15 years old _____

_____

20 years old _____

_____

40 years old _____

_____

Whether you realize it or not, decisions you make in your teens can affect your whole life. You will decide about your future training and education and how you will cope with social issues and friendships. You will have to deal with love, and, quite possibly, drugs or alcohol.

Pressure from peers makes decision making more difficult. The following responses are often heard when teen-agers attempt to influence someone else's moral decision.

"Come on, you're not a kid anymore!"
"Everybody's doing it!"
"If you loved me you would."
"Are you chicken?"

While you are learning and growing, you may not have had enough experience to make informed decisions. Gradually, it will get easier. Ideally, you will learn to consider logical alternatives. Yet, even then, you may be tempted to rely on feelings, or pressures from others. Usually a combination of factors will affect your decisions. However you do it, decision making can't be avoided.

Not Deciding is Making a Decision

Can you explain why this statement is true? A few examples might help.

Young adults who are sexually active but who have avoided deciding to use birth control methods have made a decision. They have decided to risk pregnancy and parenthood.

By not registering to vote, or by not learning enough about the candidates and issues to know how to vote, you make a decision. Your unspoken decision is to let others choose the candidate and issues for you, to give up your right to influence the election.

Your Explanation,

_____

_____

_____

_____

_____

Decisions are made in hopes of bringing about a desired goal. The following four-step procedure will assist you in making decisions that will help you achieve your goal.

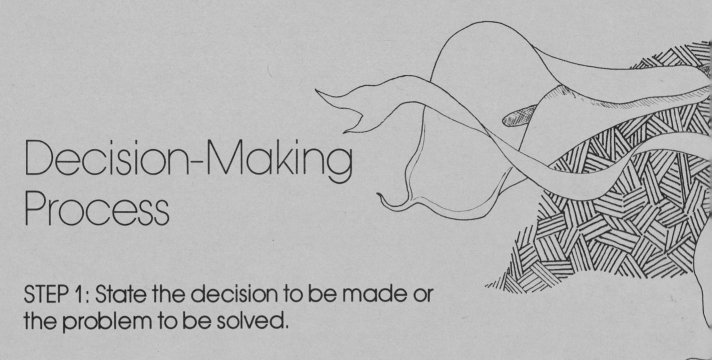

Decision-Making Process

STEP 1: State the decision to be made or the problem to be solved.

The first step is to state the decision to be made or the problem to be solved. In Sandy's case, for example, the decision to be made was to choose the classes for the next year in school.

Whenever a decision involves planning for the future, it is helpful to examine the decision in terms of stated goals.

The decision or problem: What classes should Sandy take?

Sandy's goals: To graduate from high school at the end of her senior year.

To take as many classes as possible in subjects she enjoys.

Sandy can now begin to approach decision making in terms of achieving her goals. Note that her stated goals are not the only possibilities. She also has the following options:

1. Take the easiest classes.
2. Take the classes in which she will learn the most.
3. Meet the college entrance requirements.
4. Take classes with her friends.

Sitting down to examine the problem, Sandy discovers her task is not as unpleasant as she expected. She finds that in order to graduate from high school she needs to take math, English, science, and world government. That still leaves her an elective class. Her major decision, then, is to take either college preparatory classes or general classes. Even though she doesn't really know whether she wants to go to college, she decides she should take college prep classes. Sandy has made a wise decision. Keeping options open is very important because it provides many more choices later.

Like many decisions a person makes in life, Sandy's is not irreversible. If she decided not to take a college prep program, and later wanted to go to college, she could go to a junior college and make up some classes. Her decision would only affect the type of school she could attend and the time it would take her to finish.

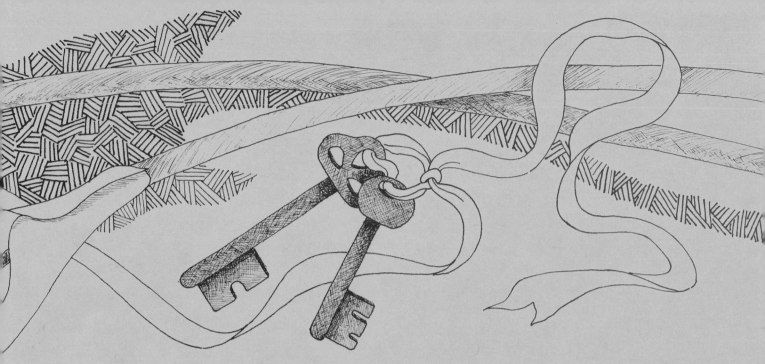

Every decision has an effect on the person who makes it but the choices are not necessarily right or wrong. Once Sandy realized that her first goal was to graduate from high school, her choices became clearer. Choosing her elective class then became the biggest problem. Her friends wanted her to work on the school paper, but she was really more interested in art or singing. She valued her friends and their opinions, but she also loved drawing and music.

Sandy stated her goal as "Choose the class I will enjoy the most." In the spaces provided, list other goals she could have chosen.

1. _____

_____

_____

2. _____

_____

_____

3. _____

_____

_____

4. _____

_____

_____

5. _____

_____

_____

STEP 2: Find and List Alternatives.

The next step toward achieving a goal or solving a problem is to list alternatives. Sandy's alternatives are to take drawing, or singing, or to work on the school newspaper. Just listing choices, in this instance, does not help her decide. Often an acceptable choice will present itself if you simply list alternatives.

The next step is to examine the advantages and disadvantages of each alternative. Here's Sandy's comparison:

Alternatives	Advantages	Disadvantages
Drawing	Enjoy the subject Would get a chance to practice techniques Like the teacher	Have taken many classes Would not be with friends
Singing	Would be part of a prestigious group Would travel and perform Enjoy singing Would see name in print	Would not be with friends Takes a lot of time Don't know teacher
School paper	Would be with friends Would learn a new skill	Don't enjoy writing Don't like the pressure of deadlines Don't know teacher

If you were in Sandy's position, which would you choose? _____

Why? _____

_____

_____

Sandy makes a decision, to eliminate the school paper. Perhaps she can deal with her friends' feelings by getting together with them at other times or by telling them how she feels.

To choose between the remaining possibilities, Sandy must consider her own values. Does she value membership in a prestigious group enough to accept the loss of free time? Only Sandy can answer that question.

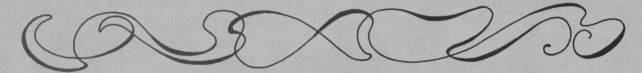

Like Sandy, you make decisions many times every day. To be successful at most of them, like deciding what to wear, what to eat, who to go out with, or where to go after school doesn't require stating your goals. Yet goals are involved just the same. To see what we mean, list four things you consider when you make the decisions listed here.

A. Deciding what to wear:

    1. _____

    2. _____

    3. _____

    4. _____

B. Deciding what to eat:

    1. _____

    2. _____

    3. _____

    4. _____

C. Deciding who to go out with:

    1. _____

    2. _____

    3. _____

    4. _____

D. Deciding where to go after school:

    1. _____

    2. _____

    3. _____

    4. _____

Now state one goal for each decision in the preceding list.

1. _____

2. _____

3. _____

4. _____

Whether or not your decisions are what most people would consider major ones, such as the choice of a college, career, or marriage partner, clarifying your thought processes by stating goals can be very helpful. Almost everything you do requires some decisions.

Lucinda's Story

Lucinda, for example, had been working at her current job for a year, and she thought she deserved a raise. Although Lucinda's supervisor had praised her, she never said anything about an increase in pay. Lucinda enjoyed her work, but she became angry every time she saw the all too familiar amount on her paycheck. What could Lucinda do to get the raise she thinks she deserves?

Lucinda's goal is to get a raise in pay. Here's her analysis of that goal.

Alternatives	Advantages	Disadvantages
Ask supervisor for raise	Will know for sure if supervisor values my work Get the raise	Supervisor may say "no" Takes courage Supervisor may be resentful
Work harder and hope someone notices	No risk involved Builds character	Time consuming Results not guaranteed Someone may not notice
Quit and look for new job	Get out of uncomfortable situation Find a better job	No job, no money May not find a job as good as this one

What Can You Do?

For this exercise we'd like you to list alternatives for each of the following situations, using Lucinda's model as an example.

DECISION 1

Tracy just moved into town, enrolled in your high school, and is in the same grade. She lives on your street, two blocks away. You know that she needs new friends to feel welcome, but for some reason she just doesn't appeal to you. You walk to school with several friends who are very happy as a group and don't really want to include anyone new. Tracy discovers you live on her street and asks if she can walk to school with you. What can you do?

What is the decision to be made? _____

_____

_____

_____

Goal? _____

_____

_____

_____

Now list your alternatives and their pros and cons.

Alternative Decisions	Advantages	Disadvantages
1.		
2.		
3.		

DECISION 2

You have been married for ten years and have three children, ages two, four, and six. You finished high school and worked for awhile as a telephone operator before your children were born. Your husband decides that he wants a divorce. You are forced to sell your house so you and your husband can divide your possessions equally. The amount of money you receive from your former husband is not enough to live on. What can you do?

What is the decision to be made? _____

_____

_____

_____

Goal? _____

_____

Alternative Decisions	Advantages	Disadvantages
1. _____		
2. _____		
3. _____		

DECISION 3

Your husband is a college dean and you are a professor of astronomy. You have been offered an important position at a university in another state. The position is at a much higher salary, and it would allow you to do work you've always wanted to do. You have two children ages 12 and 14. You know you will probably not get another chance like this. Your husband would have to take a lower-paying job if he were to move with you. What can you do?

What is the decision to be made? _____

_____

_____

_____

Goal? _____

_____

_____

_____

Alternative Decisions	Advantages	Disadvantages
1. _____		
2. _____		
3. _____		

DECISION 4

You play tennis very well and your parents want you to become a tennis pro. You enjoy tennis but do not want to expend the effort and time it would take to become a professional athlete. Your parents say it's a shame to waste your talent. They are thinking about the money you would earn. You know that not everyone with talent is actually able to be a high-salaried tennis player. What can you do?

What is the decision to be made? _____

_____

_____

Goal? _____

_____

_____

_____

Alternative Decisions	Advantages	Disadvantages
1. _____		
2. _____		
3. _____		

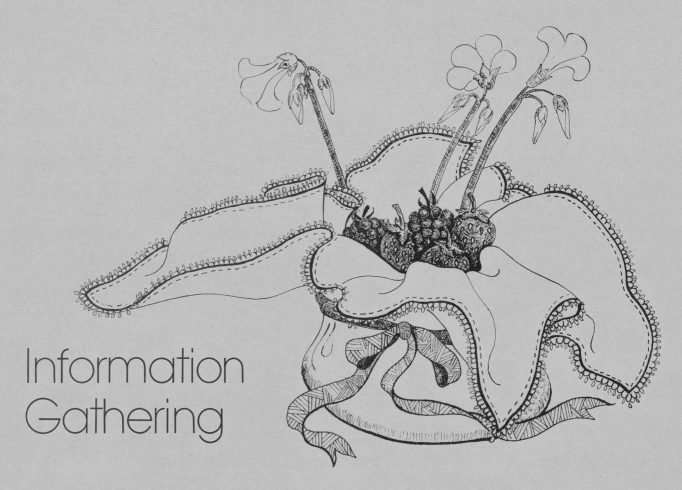

Information Gathering

Have you ever heard anyone use the term "informed decision"? It usually refers to a decision based on facts and thought, a logical decision, or perhaps the best possible decision under a particular set of circumstances.

To make an informed decision you need information — as much of it as you can get. The more information you have about a problem, the more alternatives you'll have in making a decision. That way, you're more likely to make the best decision.

The number of alternatives you were able to list for the situations in the last exercise depended mainly on the information you were given. That is why it is sometimes said that information is power. Gathering information is one of the most crucial aspects of decision making.

Before gathering information, you have to determine what you need to know. For example, Meredith is 16 years old and has been dating Sam for two years. Sam is 18 and wants to get married. Meredith wants to wait until she finishes high school. Sam works at a gas station part-time and is taking an apprentice course to be a welder.

What information do Sam and Meredith need before making their decision? _____

_____

_____

_____

_____

_____

The decision Sam and Meredith will be making is personal, yet it will probably be influenced by others. Their parents and friends, for instance, will no doubt exert strong pressures.

List some objections they might hear from parents and friends who oppose the marriage.

_____

_____

_____

_____

List some statements they might hear in favor of the marriage.

_____

_____

_____

_____

The purpose of examining pressures is to emphasize that decisions are not made in a social vacuum. Being aware of pressure helps keep it under control. This awareness is extremely important in the next step of the decision-making process. Let us look at that step right now.

STEP 3: Evaluate Alternatives.

In Step 1 you stated the decision you needed to make, or the problem you needed to solve. Then, in Step 2, you found and listed your alternatives. Step 3 in the decision-making process involves examining your alternatives. You need to find out as much about each one as you reasonably can. To gather helpful information you can read, talk to people, make observations, watch television, or do whatever is necessary. In evaluating information, always ask yourself:

1. On what basis does this person claim to know something about the topic I'm interested in?
2. Does he or she have any ulterior reason for telling me this?

In this stage of decision making, it is helpful to list how much you know about each alternative and the advantages or disadvantages of each.

For example, suppose you are thinking about whether or not you want a job after school. Your alternatives are:

1. To get a job.
2. Not to get a job.
3. Start a business.

Evaluating each alternative, you could state advantages and disadvantages like those shown here.

Alternatives	Advantages	Disadvantages
Get a job	Money Experience	Less free time Less time for school work Grades may drop
No job	More free time More time for school work Grades not likely to drop	No money No experience
Start a business	Money Experience Independence	Same as get a job

To make your decision, in light of the advantages and disadvantages of your alternatives, you need to consider:

1. The amount of free time and study time you need.
2. How important your grades are.
3. Whether or not you really need the money.
4. Whether the experience gained is likely to be helpful to you.

Listing alternatives and carefully evaluating the choices provides a framework for clear and logical thinking. Let's examine the process in working through another sample decision.

Maritza's Story

Maritza, a high school senior, has decided that she wants to go to college. Maritza has fairly good SAT scores and a 3.2 GPA. She's not sure what she'd like to major in, but she would like to live away from home. Her parents can give her some financial support, but she will need a loan or a scholarship if she wants to go to a four-year school and live on campus. A community college (two-year school) is close by. If she attended it, she could live at home and only pay for books. A state college she is considering is also in town. It has dormitories and would require minimal financial aid. Maritza has always dreamed of going to a private university. The one she has in mind is about a two-hour drive from her home, and she would need a great deal of financial aid to attend. She's worried about the difficulty of university classes even if she is accepted.

Maritza's goal: To attend college.

What are her alternatives? _____

_____

_____

What does she need to know to evaluate her alternatives? _____

_____

_____

List the advantages and disadvantages of each alternative that can be determined from what you know about the situation.

Alternatives	Advantages	Disadvantages

STEP 4: Consider the Odds.

Once you've listed alternatives and gathered and examined the information available to you, you are in the best position to know the *probable* outcome of any decision. It's rarely certain that a particular decision will lead to a desired outcome, but an informed decision can significantly improve the chances of things working out in your favor. Had Wanda used the decision-making steps, she might have saved herself some pain. Her story follows.

Wanda's Story

Wanda went on a high school skiing trip. She was a beginning skier and all her friends were better than she. She knew she should continue to take lessons but lessons were expensive. Her friends told her all she needed was a little practice and told her she should go with them to the more difficult ski runs.

Wanda's alternatives were:
1. Take lessons
2. Ski by herself on the easy slopes
3. Go with her friends

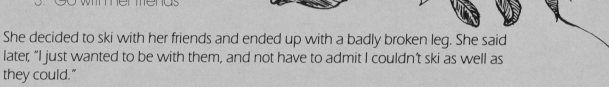

She decided to ski with her friends and ended up with a badly broken leg. She said later, "I just wanted to be with them, and not have to admit I couldn't ski as well as they could."

Looking back and examining the possible outcomes of each alternative, we see that she could have done the following:

Alternative	Probable Outcomes
Taken lessons	Learned to ski better Had less money for other things
Skied alone	Been lonely Not as much fun Improved through practice
Skied with friends	Had a great time Improved through practice Could get hurt

These were the possible results of each choice. To determine how probable they might be (to consider the odds), Wanda needed to be realistic about her skiing ability, and how difficult the slopes were. What information could she use to make these judgments?

Let's review the decision-making steps. They'll be a valuable aid to you throughout your life, whatever the decisions you need to make.

Step 1. State the goal to be achieved or the problem to be solved.
Step 2. List alternatives.
Step 3. Evaluate the alternatives.
Step 4. Consider the odds or probable outcomes.

The four steps appear simple, yet you undoubtedly know from your own experiences that making a decision is often difficult. Decisions are difficult because each of us is a complex individual with unique needs, values, and her own personality. This is why we need to learn how to gather and evaluate information.

It's time to practice making a real-life decision for yourself. In the space below, use the four-step process to make a decision about a goal you want to reach or a problem you need to solve within the next three months.

1. Decision to be made: _____

_____

Alternative	Advantages	Disadvantages	Probable Outcome
1.			
2.			
3.			
4.			

Strategies — Decision-Making Patterns[8]

There are many decision-making patterns. We'll list some in a moment that you might recognize in your own behavior. Most don't work as well as the four-step process you just learned. In fact, sometimes they can lead to disastrous results. Most of us have a tendency to use one or more of these patterns from time to time. Do you? Some of the patterns most often used are described below. See if you can think of other examples for each. Take them from your own experience, examples in this book, or any other source you'd like.

WISH PATTERN

Definition: Choosing an alternative that could lead to the most desirable result, regardless of risk.

EXAMPLE: You choose someone to marry hoping to change his bad habits.

_____

_____

_____

ESCAPE PATTERN

Definition: Choosing an alternative in order to avoid the worst possible result.

EXAMPLE: You do not go to a party because you are afraid no one will ask you to dance.

_____

_____

_____

SAFE PATTERN

Definition: Choosing the alternative that is most likely to bring success.

EXAMPLE: You take an art class knowing you are a good artist, rather than taking another subject in which you do not know how well you will do.

_____

_____

_____

IMPULSIVE PATTERN

Definition: Giving a decision little thought or examination; taking the first alternative; not looking before you leap.

EXAMPLE: You move out of your dormitory room into an apartment without first determining the advantages and disadvantages.

_____

_____

_____

FATALISTIC PATTERN

Definition: Letting the environment decide; leaving it up to fate.

EXAMPLE: You do not take the time to learn to swim before you go on a dangerous boat trip.

_____

_____

_____

COMPLIANT PATTERN

Definition: Letting someone else decide, or giving in to group pressure.

EXAMPLE: You go to a party because your friend wants to.

_____

_____

_____

DELAYING PATTERN

Definition: Postponing action and thought; procrastinating.

EXAMPLE: You leave your graduation requirements until the last semester.

_____

_____

_____

AGONIZING PATTERN

Definition: Getting so overwhelmed by alternatives that you don't know what to do.

EXAMPLE: You need to decide where you will go to college and you have so many college catalogues that you can't make up your mind.

_____

_____

_____

PLANNING PATTERN

Definition: Using a procedure so that the end result is satisfying; a rational approach.

EXAMPLE: You decide to take a job with a company with much potential for advancement.

_____

_____

_____

INTUITIVE PATTERN

Definition: Making a choice on the basis of vague feelings, or because "it feels right."

EXAMPLE: You choose a college because you like the campus. You don't talk to the instructors in your program, or find out about financial aid.

_____

_____

_____

Which pattern do you think you use the most?

_____

_____

_____

Risk Taking

Making decisions involves taking a certain amount cf risk. But then, so does *not* making a decision. There's no getting around it. Women are often called poor risk takers because they have, in the past, had a tendency to do what was safe and easy (in other words, what men and tradition said they should do). Actually, millions of women take *huge* risks every day. What, for example, could be more risky than not being able to support yourself?

It's impossible to say that risk taking, as such, is good or bad. While taking some kinds of risks is dangerous and foolish, taking others can lead to a more exciting and satisfying life. Those are the kinds of risks you want to take — the ones that can help you achieve a goal or solve a problem, without courting disaster.

Strangely enough, it may be easier to take immense risks with your financial survival than to do something you've aways wanted to do. Many people are afraid to attempt new things because they fear they will fail or look silly. Women, especially, have been brought up to "play it safe." The typical little boy may learn on the baseball field that losing is not the end of the world — there's always tomorrow. At the same time his sister may be receiving a lecture from Mom on why she shouldn't ride her bicycle in gravel; after all, she might fall and get hurt.

Such attitudes can hurt you when you start planning for a career or when you begin working. Of course you may not always get into programs you want, or maybe you won't get raises or promotions when you expect them. But that doesn't mean you shouldn't try. If you "play it safe" you have nothing to lose, but nothing to gain either. If you make an effort, you will at least be able to respect yourself for trying.

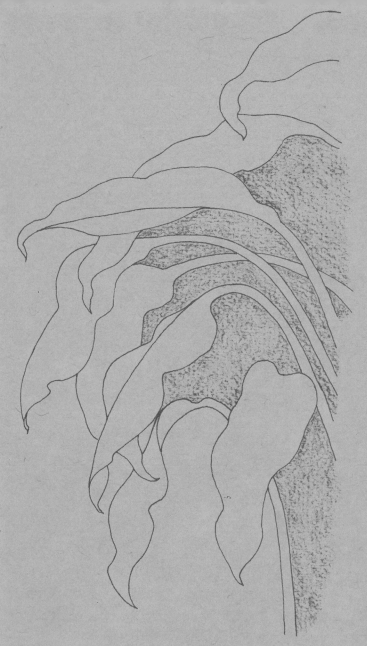

Elaine's Story

Elaine, for example, had always dreamed of being a newspaper writer. She didn't work on the school paper in high school because she was shy and she couldn't get any of her friends to join the staff with her. When she registered for her freshman year at college, Elaine saw that she could earn class credit by working on the college paper. Elaine guessed that most of the other students on the newspaper staff would have writing experience from high school. "What if I'm the worst writer in the group?" she thought to herself. But she also realized there was no way she could become a journalist without writing. She would have to either give up her dream without even trying, or she would have to take a chance and join the newspaper.

"What's the worst thing that could happen?" she asked herself. "Someone might laugh at one of my articles," she thought. "Or, the advisor might ask me to take a newswriting class to improve my skills." Finally, she decided to take the class anyway. She realized her dream was worth the risking of a little embarrassment or laughter from other staff members. Elaine accepted the risk and went to work for the college paper. Eventually, she earned a degree in journalism, and became a professional writer.

Elaine's risk wasn't a large one, yet it led to big changes in her life. Like Elaine, you will have to take some chances in order to achieve your goals. But, usually, you can break your goal into smaller, more easily managed steps that will lessen the risks involved. Taking small risks is good practice, because it will help you manage the bigger ones when they present themselves.

You can use the four-step decision-making process we have discussed to judge whether a risk is worth taking. The steps can also help you find better ways to reach your goal or solve a problem. Here are the steps again:

1. State your goal or problem
2. List your alternatives
3. Evaluate
4. Consider the odds or probable outcomes.

While we're talking about risks, it's worth noting that some risks are never worth taking. These include smoking, driving when you've been drinking, risking your health, running away from home when you have nowhere to go, hitch-hiking, not maintaining your car, leaving your house unlocked, and not preparing for your future.

Do you currently have a goal or problem which might involve some kind of risk? Are you agonizing over something that involves effort but might not be rewarded? Do you have to make a decision where there's a chance you'll lose something? Do you have to make a decision in an area in which you have limited experience? If so, use the four-step process to help you decide if you should take the risk, or, if there's a better way to get the results you want.

1. Goal to be reached or problem to be solved

_____

_____

Alternative	Advantages	Disadvantages	Probable Outcome
1.			
2.			
3.			
4.			

REFLECTIONS

Courage is the price life exacts for
granting peace.
— Amelia Earhart
Aviator

CHAPTER SIX

Getting What
You Want

Assertiveness

Assertiveness — Taking Charge of Your Life

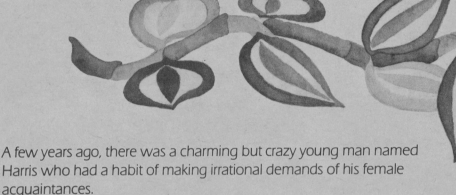

A few years ago, there was a charming but crazy young man named Harris who had a habit of making irrational demands of his female acquaintances.

"Marry me, or I'll become a topless waiter," he said to Karla one day, while the whole gang was sharing a pizza at the local hangout.

"Better you than I," replied Karla callously. "You make me want to gag."

A tear ran down Harris' cheek and dripped onto the pepperoni on his plate. Karla's friends exchanged glances which said they thought Karla was being mean and unfeeling. After all, Harris was a nice guy. And it's flattering to be proposed to, even by a "basket case." They didn't like Karla as well after that.

"Marry me, or I'll join the Foreign Legion," Harris said to Becky the next day at her locker.

"That's very flattering, Harris," Becky said, "but I don't believe in teenage marriages, and we don't really know each other that well, do we? Why don't you just walk down to the counselor's office with me? I hope we can talk you out of doing anything drastic. You're too valuable a person."

Harris was incorrigible. "Marry me, or I'll put rocks in my running shoes and go through life as a helpless cripple," he demanded of Phoebe over the phone that evening.

"Okay," said Phoebe. She honestly had no desire to marry Harris or anybody else at that time, but what could she do? His life was more important than hers, wasn't it?

Fortunately, her parents didn't agree. And since Phoebe always followed the instructions of whoever put the most pressure on her, she was saved from a disastrous marriage.

Harris, at last count, had made 497 proposals of marriage, and an equal number of ridiculous threats.

How would you handle an unwanted proposal? For years it was considered "feminine" to be like Phoebe — to give in, or to lie, rather than say what you really thought and felt. True, saying "yes" to everyone may make some people like you for awhile. Eventually there comes the day when you accept three dates for the same night, and you end up scheming, lying, and making people angry. Worst of all, *other* people seem to control your life, not you.

When they realize what is happening, many women, like Phoebe, become so angry that they lose all regard for other people's feelings, as Karla did. Becoming furious is understandable when it seems that everyone is trying to manipulate you, or that everyone is making unfair demands. Being harsh and tactless definitely lets others know what you think. But they probably won't like you or want to honor your feelings.

As is so often the case, the middle ground is the best route to take. You can be in control of your life, and still be liked and respected. The way to do it is by engaging in assertive behavior. That is, by expressing yourself honestly, but with tact and respect for the feelings of others.

You've already come a long way on the road to taking charge of your life. You've looked at who you are and how you got that way. You know what's most important to you. You can make effective decisions for yourself. You've set some goals. As you work toward these goals, you'll have to deal with all sorts of people and situations. Clearly and tactfully communicating to others what you need and expect from them will help you get what you want.

How good are you at communicating your needs? Do you let people know how you're feeling? Or do you expect them to get that information from brain waves, outer space, or your little brother, who sneaks in and reads your diary every week?

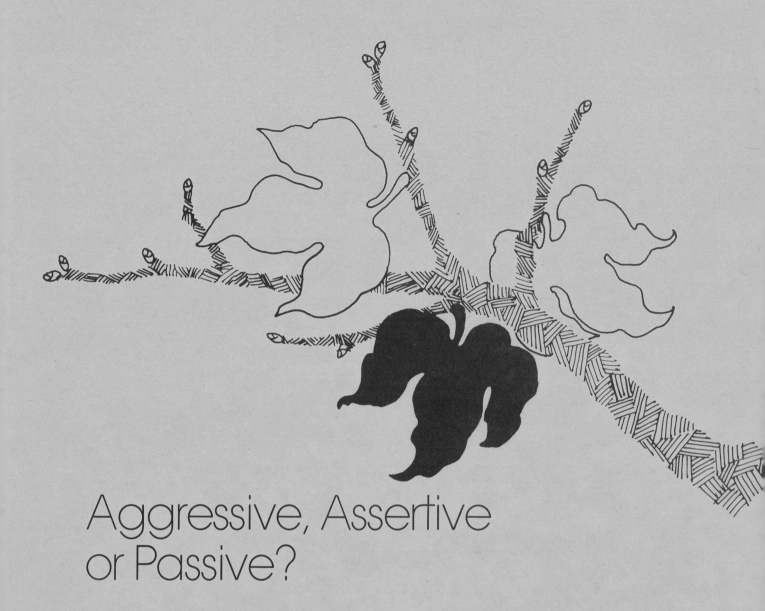

Aggressive, Assertive or Passive?

Assertiveness is a method of communication that lets others know your ideas and feelings, while respecting their feelings as well.

For the purpose of our discussion, behavior can be divided into three types: aggressive, assertive and passive. A person behaving aggressively states her feelings directly, but she violates the rights of others. For example, suppose a neighbor asks you to babysit and you don't want to. You say, "No, I won't babysit. You always ask me when I can't do it and never give me enough notice." While this may be true, your aggressive response may anger your neighbor. If it does, she probably won't ask you again. An assertive reply would be honest and direct, but not disrespectful to your neighbor. One such response might be, "No, I can't babysit, but if you would like me to come in the future, please give me about five days' notice." When you respond passively, you avoid immediate conflict, but you may be upset because you haven't expressed your feelings. A passive response to the situation would be to babysit, even though you did not want to, or to decline, by making up some excuse.

For the following examples, identify each response as: + = aggressive
0 = assertive
− = passive

SITUATION 1

You have a lot of homework and your mother asks you to do the dishes.

Response

_____ Why don't you do the dishes? Can't you see I have tons of homework?
_____ All right, Mom.
_____ I have a ton of homework tonight, and I'd rather not have to do the dishes so I can get my work finished.

SITUATION 2

Several friends at a party ask you to try drugs, but you don't want to do it.

Response

_____ Well, just this once won't hurt.
_____ You're all crazy! What do you want to do that for?
_____ No thanks, I really don't want to try drugs.

SITUATION 3

Your teacher has made a mistake grading your exam.

Response

_____ You cheated me out of ten points on this problem.
_____ I've discovered an error in the way my test was corrected.
_____ Do nothing.

SITUATION 4

Your boyfriend tells you his parents will be out of town and you can spend the evening at his house. You do not want to go, although you care for him very much. You are not busy that night.

Response

_____ My cousin's coming from out of town and I have to be with her.
_____ How can you think of doing something like that? What would happen if anyone found out?
_____ I don't feel right about doing that. Let's go to a movie instead.

SITUATION 5

Your friend wants to copy your homework and you believe that copying is wrong.

Response

_____ I worked hard on this and I want the full credit for the assignment. I don't want to take the chance of getting caught.
_____ Well, O.K. Be sure to change the words some.
_____ That's cheating.

SITUATION 6

You would like to be nominated for student council.

Response

_____ I think I am qualified and would like to be nominated for student council.
_____ Don't nominate Sarah; she's a creep.
_____ You think to yourself, I hope someone nominates me.

SITUATION 7

Someone you do not want to go out with asks you to a dance. He is the first to ask you.

Response

_____ I'm sorry, I already have a date.
_____ What? Sorry, I'm busy.
_____ Thanks for asking, but I'd rather not.

SITUATION 8

Your parents want you to attend the college they went to, but you would rather go somewhere else.

Response

_____ I'll think about what you have said, but I need to make my own decision.
_____ You always try to run my life. I've had it!
_____ If you're sure that's what is best.

SITUATION 9

You are talking to your boyfriend and suddenly realize that if you don't leave immediately you will be late for work. He wants to keep talking.

Response

_____ I really ought to be going.
_____ Oh no you don't! You're making me late for work.
_____ I know you want to talk more and we'll get together after I'm through work. Bye.

SITUATION 10

You want to enroll in auto shop but people are trying to discourage you by calling you names and making fun of you. They do not feel being a mechanic is a reasonable occupation for a woman.

Response

_____ You're all male chauvinist pigs. I can do anything you can do — only better.
_____ I want to learn to be a mechanic. You'll probably be surprised someday at what I can do.
_____ Not enroll in the class.

145

Write Your Own Responses

Get the idea? Now try the different roles.

For the following situations, write one aggressive, one assertive and one passive response. Examples of each have been done for you.

Your sister is using the telephone and you want to use it.

Aggressive: "Give me that phone!"

_____

Assertive: "I need to use the phone."

_____

Passive: Sit patiently by the phone.

_____

Your boyfriend wants to go to a movie you don't want to see.

Aggressive: "That's a dumb movie."

_____

Assertive: "I would really like to see a different movie."

_____

Passive: "If you really want to. . . ."

_____

A friend offers you pizza you don't want.

Aggressive: _____

_____

Assertive: _____

_____

Passive: _____

_____

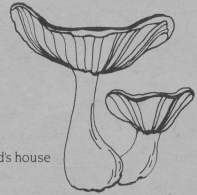

You would like another helping of food when you are a guest at a friend's house and you know there is plenty of food.

Aggressive: _____

_____

Assertive: _____

_____

Passive: _____

_____

You buy a new blouse but find a stain on it when you bring it home from the store.

Aggressive: _____

_____

Assertive: _____

_____

Passive: _____

_____

You've been standing in line for hours to buy tickets for a rock concert and someone tries to push ahead of you.

Aggressive: _____

_____

Assertive: _____

_____

Passive: _____

_____

Try to recall situations when you have responded in either an aggressive, assertive, or a passive manner. How did you feel about yourself in each situation?

Aggressive situation: _____
_____
_____
_____

How did you feel? _____
_____
_____
_____

Assertive situation: _____
_____
_____
_____

How did you feel? _____
_____
_____
_____

Passive situation: _____
_____
_____
_____

How did you feel? _____
_____
_____
_____

Truth and Consequences

The way you say things has an effect on those around you. That is why it is not always easy to respond the way you truly want. There are advantages and disadvantages in choosing an assertive, aggressive, or passive response. For example, a person may through passive behavior avoid conflicts, confrontations or risk. Passive behavior, however, may not produce the desired outcome. In the long run, overly passive persons often feel bad about themselves.

Just because you give in to someone else doesn't always mean you've been passive. It could mean you've made a conscious choice in yielding. Or, it could be because you honestly agree with the other person. Being passive refers to consistently doing things you don't really want to do.

Aggressive behavior often produces the desired outcome — at least for the moment. Releasing feelings of anger or frustration can sometimes give a person a sense of control in the situation. If, however, a person continually ignores the feelings of others, she may find herself alone and unliked.

Assertiveness allows individuals to feel good about having expressed their needs, thoughts, or feelings and about making their own choices. Assertive behavior also produces the desired result more frequently than passive behavior. However, self-assertion is not fail-safe. Note the example which follows.

Girl: "I know you'd like to go to the game, but I really don't enjoy basketball. Maybe we can go somewhere else or you can go without me."

Response 1:   Boy: (Jumps up and down.) "All right! I'll find someone who has some taste."

Response 2:   Boy: "I'm glad you told me. We can do something else — maybe a movie."

As you can see from the example, assertive responses don't always prevent unpleasant situations. Often you must decide whether or not it is wise to let others know how you feel. In the long run, though, being honest with yourself and others is beneficial to all concerned.

Assertive communication skills take practice, but they can be quite useful. By expressing yourself in ways that don't put down or offend others, you are more likely to make your point. Likewise, making your feelings known, instead of keeping them hidden, lets others know where they stand.

REFLECTIONS

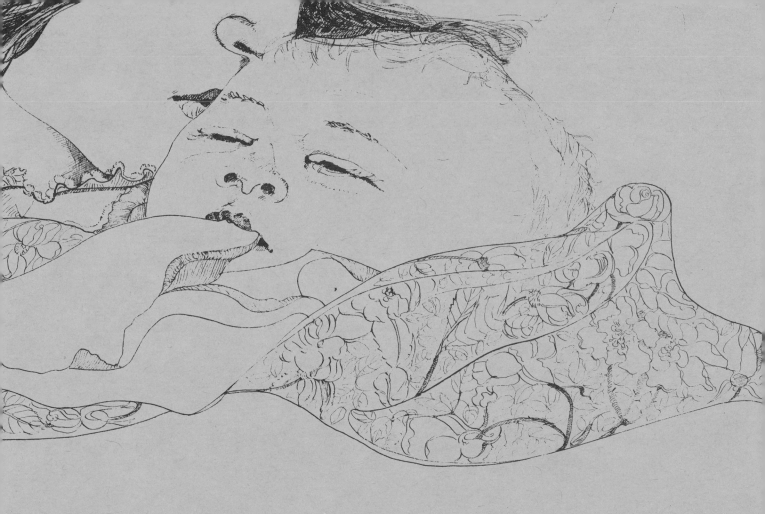

CHAPTER SEVEN

What About Marriage and Children?

Family planning

Sometimes life seems as if it involves too many decisions and too many demands. When it does, you may feel that you don't measure up. Don't despair; everyone feels pressured from time to time. That's important to remember because forgetting it can lead to the "superwoman syndrome." Later on in the chapter you'll find out what that's like, but first, we're going to talk about babies.

Whether or not to have a baby is one of the most important decisions you'll ever make. Having a baby is irreversible. Making the decision lightly or unconsciously can greatly alter not only your life, but the life of your child's father too. It may well put your baby at a serious disadvantage for his or her entire life. Compared to mothers in their twenties, teenage mothers have a 36 percent higher chance of giving birth prematurely, and their babies are 30 percent more likely to die during infancy.

There are many reasons why having a child before you're older may seem like a good idea — too many for us to discuss in detail. You owe it to yourself and your future child to choose motherhood when you can love and care for your baby responsibly. Too often, teenage mothers get pregnant because they are sad or lonely, frightened or angry.

At some point in their lives, most women do have children. The following pages will help you make the right choice at the right time.

The Egg and You

How is a baby like an egg? Well, an egg is considerably quieter and neater, not to mention cheaper; but they're both fragile. With a little imagination, you can use a common, ordinary, right-from-the-refrigerator egg to get a feeling for the responsibility and consistency needed to be a mother. The exercise you'll be doing has been used successfully in a number of schools[9]. To start, you'll need a little help from a friend or a member of your family. Have your assistant put a blue dot on the bottom of one egg, and a pink dot on the other. (Just this once, we'll go along with the stereotype: blue is for boys, pink for girls.) Pick one of the eggs from a carton in which they have been placed, dots carefully out of sight.

Congratulations! You are now the proud mother of a beautiful baby! Is it a boy or a girl? What's its name? If you like, decorate it to look more like a child before you give it a name.

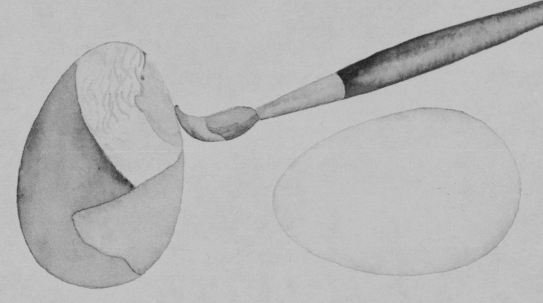

Where will you keep your newborn? Provide a place where it will be safe. Your job now is to take total responsibility for the egg-baby twenty four hours a day, for five days. At all times you must be caring for it, or it must be sleeping safely in the constant care of someone else. If you can't take it everywhere you go, you will have to find a sitter. No cheating! This is what your life would be like with a real baby.

Throughout the week, keep a journal of your activities. How do you feel about your new responsibilities? Be as realistic as possible. If you can, set your alarm clock to awaken you at 12:00 a.m., 3:00 a.m., and 6:30 a.m. just for one night. How would you feel waking up that often *every* night for baby's feeding?

Samantha did the exercise for a class project. Let's take a look at her journal.

Day One

"Congratulations to me! I am now the proud mother of a beautiful baby egg (eggette?). Her name is Sally, and I am to be her mom until classtime on Friday. I hadn't given motherhood much thought until now. Guess I'm in for quite an experience!

"Actually, I was a little disappointed with Sally at first. I sort of wanted a boy. But this is one time when you have to take what comes. And, I'm getting used to Sally. In fact, I think she looks a little like my kid brother. (Nyah, nyah, David! Serves you right if you're reading this!).

"So, anyway, I got Sally home and set up a 'crib' for her in my room. Not a minute too soon either! I'd left her in the kitchen and David and his grubby little friends were just about to escape with her for a game of catch. I put a quick end to that notion!

"And, that was just the beginning. Mom had promised to take me shopping for new shoes, but she didn't think we should take Sally. I had to find a sitter. I didn't think Lizzie would mind. She was just spending her usual three hours on the phone, anyway, and what are big sisters for? But the creep said she wouldn't babysit unless I'd do the dishes for her tonight. Bribery!

"Back at home, I was just finishing up my math homework when Mom reminded me that I hadn't given Sally any dinner. I guess real babies have a way of reminding you when they need something, but still, you have to be thinking of them all the time."

Day Two

"Sally went to school with me today, and nearly became 'eggstinct' (ha, ha). Wendy almost stepped on her while I was getting my books out of my locker, and good old practical joker Jerry spent the entire day bumping into me and hoping I'd drop her, trying to sit on her, sneaking her out of her basket when I wasn't looking, and so on. It's still hard for me to think of her constantly. Ms. Smith told us that, with real babies, you have to feed them every two and a half to four hours, and change them six to ten times a day! I complain about cleaning the cat box once a week! When I think about trying to do all that when I'm still sore and exhausted from the birth itself, I think that I won't rush into having a baby."

Day Three

"Today was neat because Mom and I had a talk about how she felt when she had us. I don't know why, but we'd never talked about it before. It made me feel really close to her. She said the first weeks were really hard. She cried a lot, and worried whether we were getting enough to eat. On top of that, her breasts were really sore until the milk supply was established (she nursed us). But it all worked out, and she says she's glad she had us. Even David.

"I'm getting better about remembering Sally, but it's not doing my social life any good. Bob asked me to go to the movies tomorrow night, but I didn't know if I could get a sitter. Mom and Dad are going to be home though, so I finally said I could go. I wonder how often I'd get to go out if I had a real baby!"

Day Four

"Today I was horrified to learn that most babies aren't toilet-trained until they're two or three years old! Yuk! Everyone says it's not as disgusting when it's your own baby, but still, I can think of more pleasant ways to spend my time — starting a cat box cleaning service, maybe?

"Seriously, it's just such a drain having this big responsibility hanging over me all the time. I didn't realize how much energy it would take!"

Day Five

"Good-bye, Sally! We gave our babies up for adoption today, and I felt a little funny about it — like giving up part of myself.

"But I have a better idea now of how much time, money, and emotion go into raising a child, and I want to make sure I'm ready before I do it for real. I realize that I'm not ready to make that commitment yet. I have a lot more things to do and accomplish before another human being can be my top priority in life.

"Someday I'll probably have a baby, but in the meantime, hello, my old friend, Freedom!"

YOUR JOURNAL

First Day

Second Day

Third Day

Fourth Day

Fifth Day

Ask a Mother

Do you know someone with a child under six months of age? Talk with her about her experiences and record her responses.

Mother's name _____ Age _____

Place of residence _____

How long married? _____

Baby's name _____ Age _____

Why did you decide to have a baby when you did? _____
_____
_____

How has the baby changed your life? _____
_____
_____
_____

What surprised you most about caring for a child? _____
_____
_____

How do you feel physically? Emotionally? _____
_____
_____

How much does your husband help with the baby? _____
_____
_____

If you had it to do over again, would you? _____
_____
_____

Having a Child is Expensive

Having and caring for a child takes money as well as commitment. How much will it cost? To get a rough idea, find the approximate prices for the services and products listed in this exercise.

The first expenses you need to consider are the costs of having a baby.

Call a local obstetrician and a hospital; then fill in the costs below.

Average Maternity Costs
Prenatal care and delivery:

Doctor _____

Hospital _____

TOTAL _____

Find the cost of maternity clothes.

_____

_____

_____

_____

_____

_____

Newborns require a lot of equipment. Find the cost of the items on the following list by visiting local stores, checking newspaper ads, or asking someone who has recently purchased the items.

Crib	_____
Crib bumper	_____
Crib sheets	_____
Mattress cover	_____
Stroller	_____
High chair	_____
Infant seat	_____
Playpen*	_____
Diapers (box of 36)	_____
Blankets	_____
Undershirts	_____
Sleepers	_____
Plastic pants	_____
Dress-up clothes	_____
Bottles	_____
Bibs	_____
Car Seat	_____
Dressing table*	_____
Toys	_____
Miscellaneous	_____
Other	_____
TOTAL	_____

* optional

Researchers tell us it costs over $200,000 to raise a child in today's world. Of course, that's spread out over many years — but it is a sizeable financial commitment. Not being prepared to meet that commitment may strain a marriage and is often responsible for break-ups. Being financially ready to have a child just makes good sense.

Money is only one part of the preparation for having a baby. Thinking very seriously about how your life would be changed by a child is another. What would happen to you if you were to have a baby now? Brenda, Karen, Barbara and Rochelle described what happened to them.

Brenda's Story

"I am 16 years old and pregnant. I just really didn't think it could happen to me. I thought Jerry loved me. He kept saying he did and that I should trust him. I trusted him all right, but now what am I going to do? He's really freaking out. We don't want to get married. I'm only 16 and so is he. We don't believe in abortion and I don't want to give the baby up for adoption. How can I keep it? Jerry's going to school. My parents are so mad and my friends—what can they do? I've spent the last week crying practically all the time. What am I going to do?"

Karen's Story

"I had Jonathan when I was 15. My boyfriend left when he found out I was pregnant and so I'm raising the baby alone, with help from my mom. It's really hard getting through the days. There's no time to go out—just work and school and taking care of the baby. No one wants to go out with a mother. I wish I could live my life over. But I can't, so I've got to see it through. Don't get me wrong, I love my baby, but. . . ."

Barbara's Story

"Tim and I got married right after high school. Becky was born one year later. Everyone said we were too young to have kids, but we wanted a child and we're happy. The biggest problem right now is money. Tim has to work to support Becky and me, but he'd like to go to City College to get training as an auto mechanic so he could get a higher paying job. I can't go to work because the kind of job I'd get would hardly pay for the sitter. Besides I want to stay home. It's really hard."

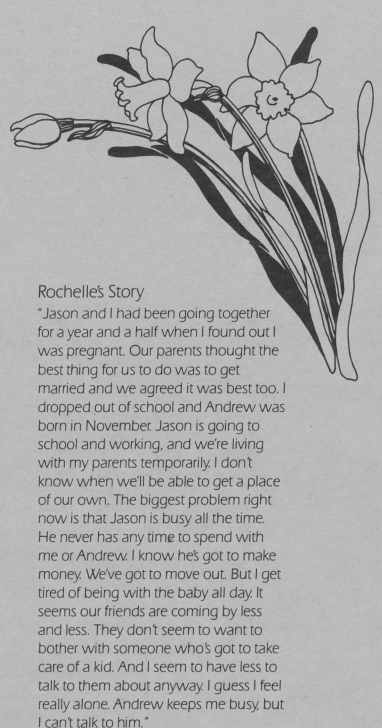

Rochelle's Story

"Jason and I had been going together for a year and a half when I found out I was pregnant. Our parents thought the best thing for us to do was to get married and we agreed it was best too. I dropped out of school and Andrew was born in November. Jason is going to school and working, and we're living with my parents temporarily. I don't know when we'll be able to get a place of our own. The biggest problem right now is that Jason is busy all the time. He never has any time to spend with me or Andrew. I know he's got to make money. We've got to move out. But I get tired of being with the baby all day. It seems our friends are coming by less and less. They don't seem to want to bother with someone who's got to take care of a kid. And I seem to have less to talk to them about anyway. I guess I feel really alone. Andrew keeps me busy, but I can't talk to him."

What changes might happen in your life if you were expecting a baby nine months from now?

What Do I Really Want?

Deciding whether or not to marry and then whether or not to have children are very important choices with large consequences. Ask yourself the following questions when wrestling with these decisions.

What do I want out of life for myself? _____

_____

_____

Am I ready to marry? _____

Have my husband-to-be and I discussed our views on work, religion, children and future goals?

_____

Would having children fit in with our plans? _____

_____

What if we have a child and then discover that we made a wrong decision?

_____

_____

Can we afford a child? _____

Do we know what it costs in money and energy to raise a child?

_____

Do we like children and enjoy spending time with them?

_____

How do we get along with our parents now?

_____

_____

Will our parents be able to help us with child care?

_____

If I were left alone, could I be the main source of support, both emotional and financial, for a child?

_____

What Causes Unplanned Pregnancies?

The majority of teenage mothers did not plan to conceive children in their teens. Some pregnancies are the result of ignorance. Others occur because the people involved think, "It won't happen to me." Some happen because the girl is unwilling to admit what she is really doing. "He made me do it," or, "I was drunk." Still others occur because the girl, hoping to keep the love or friendship of the boy, is afraid to deny his desires. A girl under such pressures sometimes shows poor judgment or doesn't know how to respond.

What do you think are the major reasons for unplanned pregnancies?

_____

_____

_____

Create an assertive response that a girl could use to protect her rights and her body in each of the following situations:

Boyfriend: "If you loved me, you would!" _____

_____

_____

Boyfriend: "You're not a little girl anymore." _____

_____

_____

Boyfriend: "Everyone else is doing it." _____

_____

_____

Boyfriend: "We'll only go so far." _____

_____

_____

Babies Have Fathers Too

You may have thought a lot about what your ideal man will look like. What about his other attributes? Have you thought about them?

The list you see here gives some possible characteristics. Circle the five that are most important to you at this point in your life, and cross out the five that seem the least important.

I would like my future husband to have:

Good looks
An impressive job
A good sense of humor
Similar religion
Same values
Similar goals
Common interests
The ability to communicate
   well with me
Other _____

_____

A college degree
A fancy car
Good taste
Optimism and confidence
Interesting friends
Eyes only for me
A fondness for dancing
Money
Other _____

_____

I would like my future husband to be:

Considerate
Wealthy
Kind
Aggressive
A good provider
Talented
Strong
Attractive physically
Happy-go-lucky
Macho
Other _____

_____

Undemanding of me
Punctual
Full of surprises
Intelligent
Hard-working
Devoted to me
Successful
Nonsexist
Forgiving
Well-dressed
Other _____

_____

However you make your decision about who to marry, remember, it is an important one. When the time comes, be sure to consider all your options, including the option of not marrying at all.

Having a child at any age isn't easy. Imagine that you and your husband just sat down to dinner. He had a hard day's work at the office. You are fairly exhausted from carrying a crying baby, changing diapers, bathing the baby, trying to clean the house, trying to prepare meals, and doing two washes because the baby spit up all over everything. The baby is finally napping. Suddenly, just as the two of you settle down to enjoy dinner, the baby starts to scream.

Rate each of the following responses. Place an "A" by the one you think most commonly occurs in households across the country and an "F" by the one least common. Use the letters "B" through "E" to rank the others from "most common" to "least common."

1. John: "Darling, the baby's crying. Why don't you see if she's hungry?"
2. Both Parents: Try to ignore the crying while the tension increases and the meal looks less pleasant.
3. John: "Why does she always start screaming when I get home? Can't you do something with her?"
4. Sue: "It's your turn. I've been working all day."

    John: "But I've been working all day too. Don't I get any break? Coming home sure is a joy."
5. Sue: "I've tried everything. She's been fed and changed and the doctor says she's not sick. I don't know what to do anymore." (Begins crying.)
6. John: "Darling, I hear the baby. I'll go see if I can figure out what's bothering her."

Teri and Ben

Teri and Ben had talked about having a family some day. When they were first married their parents hinted subtly, "Did you see the Smith's darling grandchildren?" Nonetheless, Teri and Ben decided they should wait a few years to make sure they could really afford a child. They wanted to get to know each other, too. They had heard that having a baby can be a "crisis" point in a marriage, so they wanted to make sure their relationship was strong enough to survive.

"I'm really glad we waited," said Teri. "Michelle is everything we hoped for, but nobody can make you understand beforehand how difficult being a parent is. Our whole lives have changed. We have to plan everything we do now and Ben complains nothing is spontaneous anymore—except when the baby spits up all over me as we're about to go out. But by the time we had Michelle we could really talk to each other and work things out. We were ready."

Knowing you can expect major changes in your life is an important part of deciding whether or not to start a family. It is information you need to consider in evaluating your alternatives. Thinking through the steps of the decision-making process can bring the issues involved more clearly into focus. Review the steps listed on page 133.

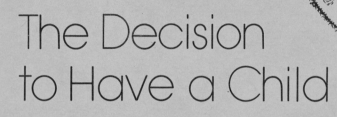

The Decision to Have a Child

STEP 1 State goal or problem to be solved.
      a. Whether or not to have a child.

STEP 2 List alternatives.
      a. To have a child.
      b. Not to have a child.

STEPS 3 & 4 Evaluate alternatives and consider the odds.

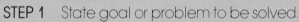

Alternative	Advantages	Disadvantages	Probable Outcome
To have a child.	Joy of children Sharing with another person New experiences Other _____ _____	Fewer options for your future Increased financial burden Increased responsibilities Commitment Less time for yourself Other _____ _____	Will definitely have new experiences, increased financial burden, increased responsibilities May have joy
Not to have a child.	Independence Greater financial resources More flexibility Other _____ _____	Possible loneliness in old age Miss out on immediate family experience Other _____ _____	Will have more independence and flexibility May be lonely

One consequence of not having a child now is that you may have to make that decision again at a later date. How will you decide? Use the decision-making steps shown here to help decide, "When should I have children?"

STEP 1 State the problem to be solved.

When should I have children? _____

_____

_____

_____

STEP 2 List alternatives. (Examples: When I'm 25, when I'm established in my career, when I've been happily married for two years.)

1. _____

2. _____

3. _____

4. _____

STEPS 3 & 4 Evaluate alternatives and consider the odds.

Alternative	Advantages	Disadvantages	Probable Outcome
1.			
2.			
3.			
4.			

What About Your Goals?

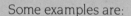

Now that you know what to consider when deciding about having children, your final choice rests on your goals and values. What factors are most important to you? Independence? The joy of being closely associated with others? Think about your goals as they relate to having children.

Some examples are:

1. My goal is to have two children when I'm happily married in my late twenties, after establishing a career.
2. I plan not to have children.
3. I would like to have two children in my twenties and stop work for a period of six years after the birth of my children.
4. Ideally, I will have one child in my early thirties and continue working at my career.
5. I'm hoping to have a child as soon as possible.

In the space provided, write your present goal with respect to having children, and two objectives to help you reach it.

Today my goal with respect to having children is: _____

_____

_____

_____

Objectives:

1. _____

_____

2. _____

_____

166

Child Care

Since having children can have a major impact on your career, be sure to consider your values regarding family and child care. Do you think it's important for a mother to stay home during her child's early years? If so, is the career you selected one that would allow you to return to work after an absence of several years without losing status or seniority? Could you afford to live on your husband's income alone during these years?

Today many women find it necessary to return to work three to six months after giving birth because they need the money. As a result, there are more options available for child care than there used to be. Day-care centers provide trained and reliable caretakers for a child while you are at work. Many corporations are providing day-care centers for their employees' children. This makes it easier for parents to drop off and pick up their pre-schoolers. Fathers are taking a more active part in child care. Parents with high paying jobs may be able to have full-time help at home.

Could your husband's job be flexible so the two of you could share child care chores? How would you feel about such an arrangement? How would he feel? Would you feel guilty about leaving your child with a sitter? Would staying at home with a young child be too confining for you so you'd like to continue working part-time or full-time? What are your values?

What child care resources exist in your community? Would you feel comfortable using them? Write your thoughts here.

_____

_____

_____

_____

Your values will change and should constantly be re-examined in order to help you make decisions.

Despite the problems, most people find that the joys of having children make up for all the sacrifices. The better prepared you are, the more you will know what to expect. And the more you know your goals, values, capabilities, and desires, the more likely you are to make the best decision for you and your child.

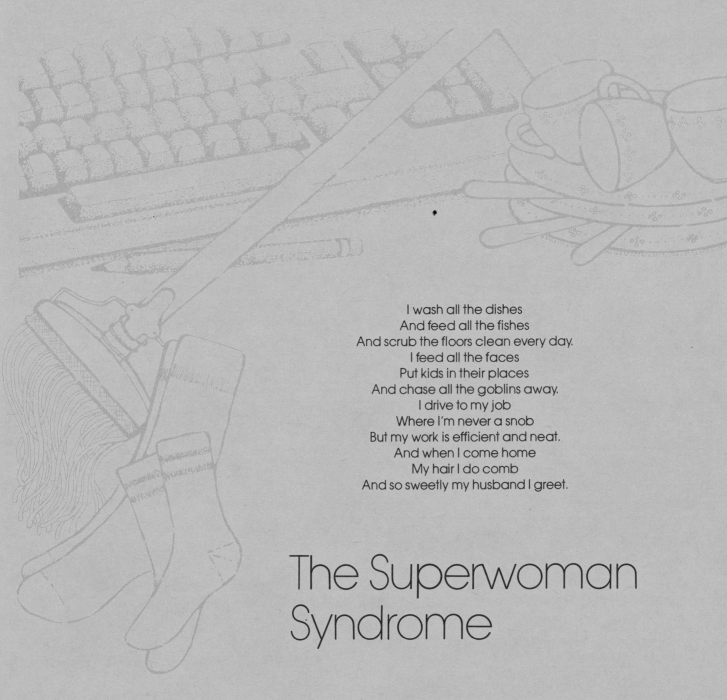

I wash all the dishes
And feed all the fishes
And scrub the floors clean every day.
I feed all the faces
Put kids in their places
And chase all the goblins away.
I drive to my job
Where I'm never a snob
But my work is efficient and neat.
And when I come home
My hair I do comb
And so sweetly my husband I greet.

The Superwoman Syndrome

How realistic is that picture? Can you really "have it all now"? Judging from TV and the movies, "Superwoman" is alive and well. You know the one, the fashionably dressed, perfectly made-up mother of four who runs a million-dollar business in her spare time. That is, when she's not lecturing at Harvard, advising Congress on how to avert national disaster or appearing on a TV talk show to tell us all how to use our food processors during natural childbirth. Of course, she wouldn't *think* of letting her husband help with the housework.

Well, there is no such woman. Thank goodness! You cannot have everything, do everything, and be everything, all at the same time. Priorities have to be set. Working mothers need help from their families. They may have to accept the fact that their homes will not always pass the "white glove test." Maintaining a strong marriage, happy and healthy kids, and a career you enjoy are realistic goals as long as you keep in mind that things will never be perfect.

Setting Priorities and Making Time

If you can't have *everything*, what can you have? Well, what do you want? What do you want *most*? It might be painful to find that "you're only human," but at least you have the power to decide which things are most important to you. Then you can make those goals your top priorities — the things you'll try hardest for, put ahead of other interests, spend the most time on. It's possible to have hundreds of accomplishments and still find yourself unsatisfied, simply because you never made time to do the one thing you most wanted. The next exercise will help you decide what your priorities are and where your time can best be spent.

"Superwoman's" list of activities has already been completed. After reading it, use the spaces provided to make a list of all the things you have to do or would like to do in the following week. Include schoolwork, outside jobs, chores at home, activities with friends, whatever you usually do. Then, beside each entry, indicate its importance to you. Many factors contribute to how "important" each task is. For example, washing the dishes may not be *personally* important to you, but cooperating with your parents' requests may be.

For each task or activity, indicate its importance by writing an "A", "B", or "C". Place an "A" by activities that *have* to get done in the next week or are of most importance for you personally. You will sacrifice some things for these. They are your top priorities. Then write a "B" by activities that are important, but not crucial. Write a "C" by items that would be nice to get done if you have time, but won't cause problems if they are left undone.

After you have listed your "A", "B", and "C" priorities, try to work on your "A's" first and complete them before going on to the "B's". Then finally, if you have the time, do your "C" tasks.

Our fictitious (and over-extended) "Superwoman's" list might look something like this:

Return proofs of new book to publisher	— A	Take flying lesson	— B
Interview with Barbara Walters	— A	Cammie's Little League game	— A
Change oil on Mercedes	— C	Run in Boston Marathon	— A
Conference with kids' teachers	— A	Weed vegetable garden	— B
Dinner with John Travolta	— B	Repair home computer	— B
Clean toilets	— C	Paint mural on front hall wall	— C
Read newspaper	— C	Iron sheets	— C
Testify before Senate committee	— A	Wax no-wax floor	— C
Bake brownies	— C	Start research for new book	— B
Sew costume for Muffy	— A	Romantic evening with Tom	— A
Attend exercise class	— C	Sleep	— C

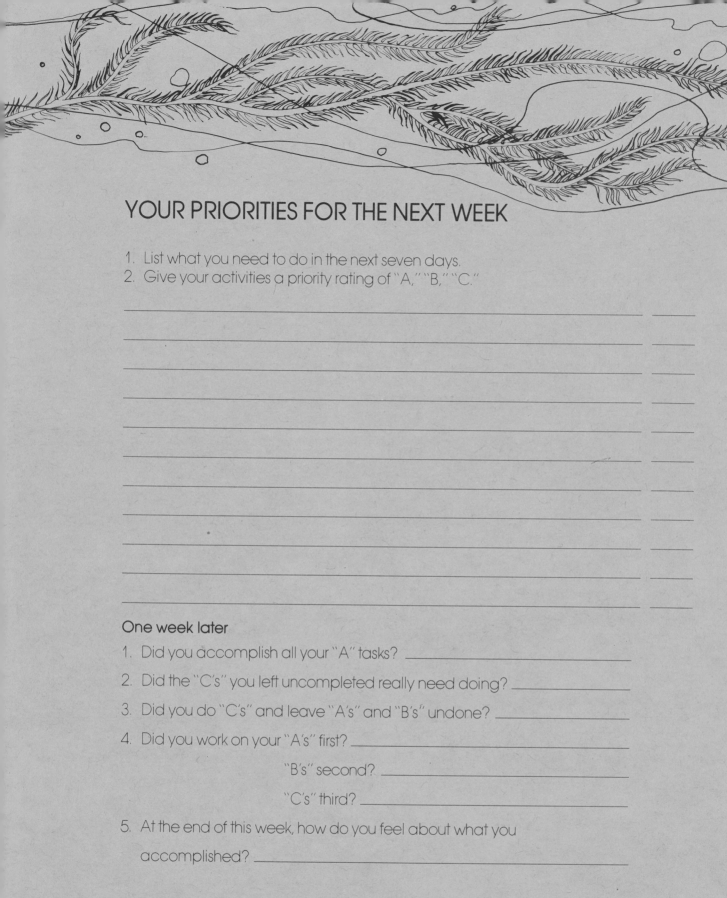

YOUR PRIORITIES FOR THE NEXT WEEK

1. List what you need to do in the next seven days.
2. Give your activities a priority rating of "A," "B," "C."

_____ _____

_____ _____

_____ _____

_____

_____

_____

_____

_____

_____

_____

_____ _____

One week later

1. Did you accomplish all your "A" tasks? _____

2. Did the "C's" you left uncompleted really need doing? _____

3. Did you do "C's" and leave "A's" and "B's" undone? _____

4. Did you work on your "A's" first? _____

   "B's" second? _____

   "C's" third? _____

5. At the end of this week, how do you feel about what you

   accomplished? _____

A list like this allows you to plan your time more effectively, achieve the things that are most important to achieve at the time, and helps you avoid procrastination of an important, but maybe unpleasurable activity.

YOUR PRIORITIES FOR THE NEXT MONTH

1. List what you need to do during the next month.
2. Give your activities a priority rating of "A," "B," "C."

_____   _____
_____   _____
_____   _____
_____   _____
_____   _____
_____   _____
_____   _____
_____   _____
_____   _____
_____   _____
_____   _____
_____   _____
_____   _____
_____   _____
_____   _____
_____   _____
_____   _____
_____   _____
_____   _____
_____   _____
_____   _____
_____   _____

REFLECTIONS

If you don't know where you're
going . . . you're there.

CHAPTER EIGHT

What Can You Do?

Skills identification

Sarah Crocker's Story

"I don't know what to do," said Sarah Crocker to her friend Louise. "I'm supposed to identify all my skills for my career planning class, and it makes me feel like such a loser! I mean, I can't do anything! Want another piece of cheesecake?"

"Sure," said Louise. "This is great stuff!"

"Thanks. I've got about a zillion of them here. My mom's club is having its annual bazaar tomorrow, and people have been calling all week to reserve them. I made a bunch last year, and they were sold out in about five minutes. So I've been making cheesecake for days, and I haven't even had time to think about my skills. My list is due Monday. Mrs. Johnson is going to kill me!"

Sometimes it's hard to see the obvious. Fortunately for Sarah Crocker, her teacher, Mrs. Johnson, arrived at the bazaar early enough to buy one of Sarah's cheesecakes, and launched her on a very successful career. Sarah Crocker Frozen Cheesecakes are now available in all fifty states and twenty countries. Sarah is currently negotiating a contract to distribute them in China.

What about you and your skills? If you've thought about them at all, you've probably underestimated yourself. Whether you're making a cheesecake or solving a math problem, everything you do involves a skill. And, for most people, what you do with your life depends on what you do well.

It's time to start looking at yourself in terms of what you like to do and what you are able to do. A word of caution here, before you start. This won't work unless you're realistic. *No one person is good at everything, nor is there any person devoid of all skills.* Strengths and weaknesses vary from person to person. There are over 20,000 different jobs. Some of them are right for you.

If you aren't successful at making things, if solving math problems is frustrating and takes you a long time, if you can't run fast, whatever your weaknesses are, take a minute to ask yourself why you have difficulty with some tasks. Is a lack of experience or ignorance the problem? Or is this simply not one of your strengths?

If you honestly feel you don't have the aptitude to be really good at something, don't feel that you should give it up entirely. If it's something you enjoy, that's great. Keep it up. It's smart to avoid trying to make a living at a job that requires a skill you simply don't have. With that caution, it's time to look at what you can do.

What Are Your Skills?

Like many people, when Miranda thought about skills, she thought of things like designing computers or playing tennis with both legs tied together, using a shovel instead of a racquet, as she had seen on TV. (Now there's a skill!) She never considered the things she did every day as skills. But in a typical day she might get an "A" on a math test, sell eighteen boxes of candy to raise money for the band, turn down a date with Tom (she already had a date) in a way that would encourage him to ask her again, type a history paper, make dinner for the family, and put together a terrific outfit for Cindy's party. All of Miranda's activities involve skills. And so do *your* activities. Not only do you already know how to do hundreds of things, but you have the potential to learn many more.

As you go through your day, jot down the things that you do and the skills that they involve. You may be surprised at the variety of your talents. Use the following exercise to help identify them.

List as many of your activities as you can think of (playing piano, ice skating, bike riding, typing, organizing a class party, introducing two friends you think have something in common, etc.) on the chart which follows.

What kinds of skills are involved in each activity? Record them in the "Skills" column on the chart.

Next, think about what it is that you *like* about each of the activities. Do you enjoy bike riding because you're faster than any of your friends? Because you like to look at the countryside? Some other reasons? List your likes in the "What Do You Like About This Activity?" column on the chart.

In what *environment* are the activities conducted? Indoors? With people? Alone? List the environments in the "Environment" column on the chart.

Activities	Skills	What Do You Like About This Activity?	Environment

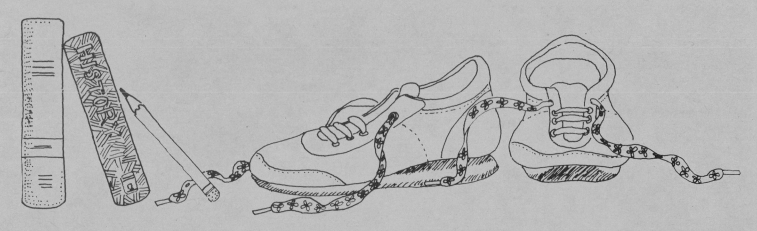

What about school? What are your best subjects? Your worst? What is your favorite? Why? Make sure your reactions are to the *subject*, not just to a teacher you particularly like or dislike. If you're not really sure what you like, you might want to ask your school counselor about interest inventory tests. She or he should be able to help you with this. An interest inventory is a quick-answer test that, when evaluated, helps give insight into where your interests lie. You may discover some interests you haven't considered at all.

Best subjects: _____

_____

_____

_____

Why? _____

_____

_____

_____

Worst subjects: _____

_____

_____

Why? _____

_____

_____

_____

Favorite subjects: _____

_____

_____

Why? _____

_____

_____

_____

Job Skills

All jobs require some skills. The ability to work quickly with numbers or information is required by many jobs. Being able to talk to people, to influence them or supervise them is an important skill in many occupations. The ability to maneuver an earth-mover or operate a complicated machine is still another skill area required by many jobs. One could say that some jobs require "people skills," others rely more on manual dexterity and working with things, and still others require manipulating numbers, data or ideas. Miranda's selling candy and dealing diplomatically with Tom are "people skills." Typing, making dinner and coordinating her party outfit are skills that deal with things. Miranda has math ability as well.

Look back at your own list of skills. Do they seem to be more prevalent in one or two areas? Do you have a preference for dealing with people? Information? Things? When you learn something new, ask yourself how it relates to a skill. If you seem to come up with a number of skills that involve talking with people, and if you enjoy it, that can be a valuable clue as to what your career might be. What kinds of jobs involve talking with people? A marriage counselor, a psychologist, or a principal are a few possible choices. Use the types of skills that stand out on your own list and think of as many jobs as you can that might relate to each. For example, Miranda's success at selling candy could indicate that she'd be good at selling real estate, as well. Or her diplomacy could be developed into a job with the foreign service. What about your skills?

_____

_____

_____

_____

_____

_____

_____

_____

_____

_____

Experience What You Can

If you still think your list of skills looks a little sparse, don't worry. You're young. There are thousands of things you haven't had a chance to experience yet. It's not too soon to start. The more experiences you have, the better able you'll be to make career decisions. The opportunities are there. At school, there are sports to be played, organizations to be joined, and unusual classes to be taken. Try out for choir or a school play, if you think you might enjoy it; or work on the newspaper. If you live in a city, visit its museums — most offer free admission on certain days of the week. Many theatres offer low rates to students. Summer jobs can provide a wide variety of experiences. Run for student council, or work on a political campaign. Get to know people of different ages and cultural backgrounds, and learn from them. Even if you tend to be shy, joining a club or taking part in activities will put you in contact with other people who have similar interests. You'll find that the more things you try, the bolder you will become. The whole world will open up to you!

If you're particularly attracted to a certain environment (the beach, a hospital), spend time there. Look around. What are people doing on the job? Do any of the jobs appeal to you? Be bold! Ask questions! Your future could depend on it!

REFLECTIONS

CHAPTER NINE

Why Not Be a Plumber, Jockey, or Engineer?

Non-traditional careers

The wave of the future is coming
and there is no stopping it.
— Anne Morrow Lindbergh,
    Writer

Modern invention has banished the
spinning wheel, and the same law of
progress makes the woman of today
a different woman from her
grandmother.
— Susan B. Anthony

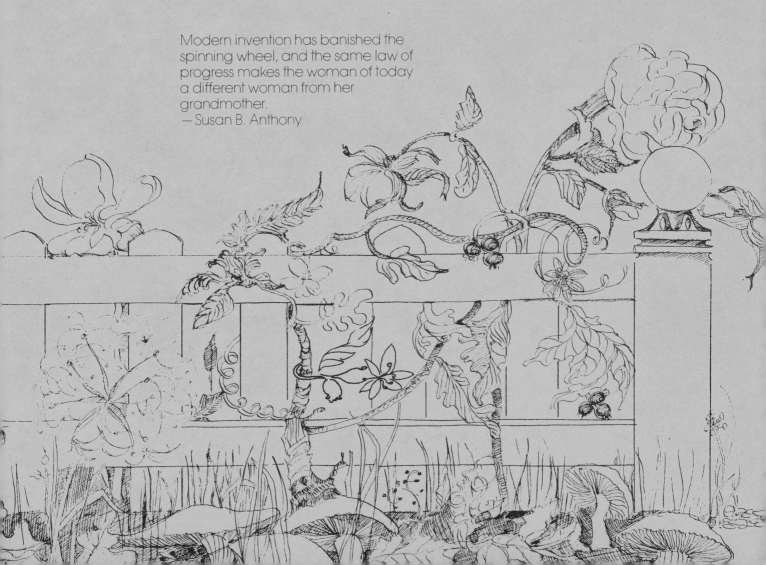

Rose's Story

Once upon a time, before there were stereo headsets or acrylic fingernails, there lived a girl named Rose. One day, she bravely announced to all her friends who were planning to be secretaries, "I want to be a plumber."

"A plumber!" exclaimed her father. "What kind of job is that for a girl? You'll get dirty! You'll hurt yourself!"

"It can't be any nastier than changing diapers," said Rose, who had been babysitting for years. "I have the ability. I want to do it." She raised her voice for emphasis, and would not change her mind, even when her father offered bribes of cashmere sweaters and a trip to Hawaii.

"A plumber!" cried her mother. "What will people say? Why can't you be nice like your cousin Ruth who's doing so well as a typist, and gets to wear high heels and earrings and to make coffee for all those important men at the bank?"

"I'd rather make money than coffee," insisted Rose, as she refused to change her mind and handed her mother a handkerchief for her tears. "It'll be all right, Mom. Someday you'll be proud of me."

And Rose was right. After starting work as a plumber, she not only felt she was doing what she wanted, but soon she was making over $13 an hour. Later, she started her own business, and before long, had several franchises. Pink "Plumbing by Rose" vans could be seen making house calls in towns throughout her part of the country. Soon after, Rose bought herself a sports car and sent her parents on a trip to Hawaii.

Cousin Ruth, in the meantime, was still wearing high heels and earrings to her job at the bank, where she was still making the coffee—and still making less than a quarter of what Rose made when she started.

Thanks to Rose and lots of other brave women, it is easier for you to work as a plumber, lawyer, pilot, or anything else that not so long ago you had to be a man to be. It still may not be *easy* to pursue such careers, but the ice has been broken in most fields. You will probably never have to be "The First Woman" anything. (If your heart is set on being the first woman in some particular occupation, however, there are still a few career choices remaining. President of the United States is one you may want to tackle.)

Why should you consider careers that have been traditionally held by men? There are a couple of good reasons. The first is that, in general, you will be able to make more money at them. Look back at your budget. It costs a lot to support yourself today. Many of the so-called "women's jobs" just do not pay enough for a person to live on.

And secondly, you may find "male" jobs as interesting and fulfilling as many of the men who hold them do. Just like boys, you have talents and abilities of different kinds. Why shouldn't you be able to put them to use in the way that will make you happiest? You owe it to yourself to consider *all* possibilities before you make your career choices.

Ask a Career Woman

What do the working women you know think about career choices? Interview two who are close to you, using these questions as a guide.

First Interview

Person interviewed _____

Job title _____ Date _____

Why did you choose the career you did?

_____

_____

_____

What has been the most satisfying part of your job?

_____

_____

_____

What has been the least satisfying, or the most frustrating part
of your job?

_____

_____

_____

If you had to do it over, would you choose the same job?

_____

If not, what other choice would you make?

_____

As a young woman ready to start preparing myself for a career, what advice would you give me?

_____

_____

_____

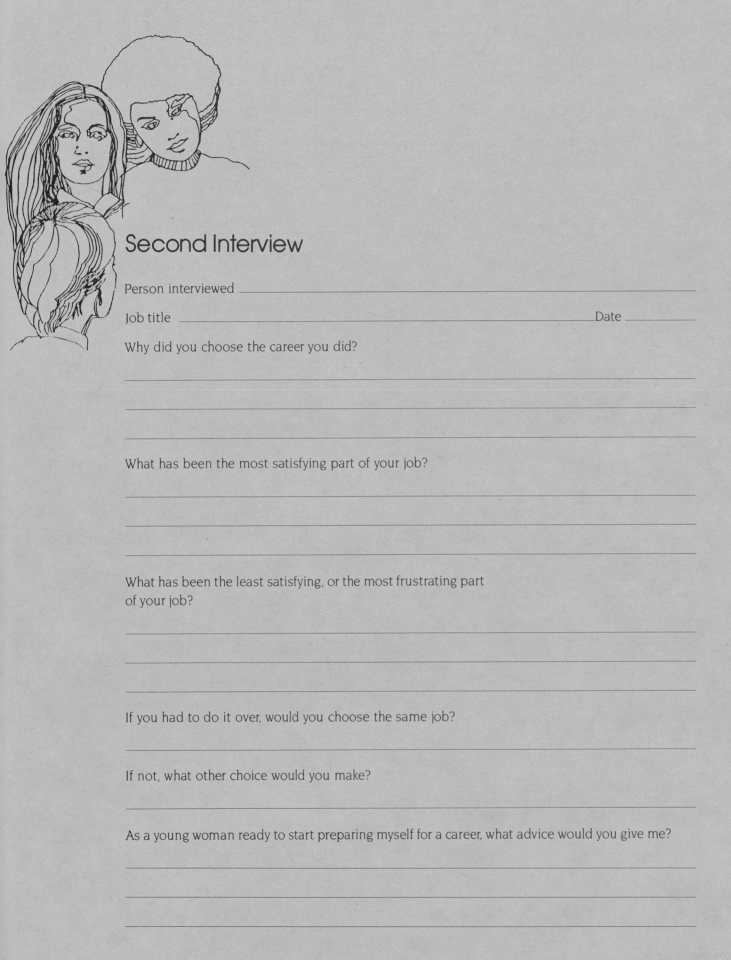

Second Interview

Person interviewed _____

Job title _____ Date _____

Why did you choose the career you did?

_____

_____

_____

What has been the most satisfying part of your job?

_____

_____

_____

What has been the least satisfying, or the most frustrating part
of your job?

_____

_____

_____

If you had to do it over, would you choose the same job?

_____

If not, what other choice would you make?

_____

As a young woman ready to start preparing myself for a career, what advice would you give me?

_____

_____

_____

Women have made many advances in recent years. The following table lists just a few of their "firsts." New "firsts" are now less common, because so many women have entered careers that were formerly thought to be "for men only."

SOME FEMALE FIRSTS

First woman to pilot a jet plane	Ann Baumgartner 1947
First woman U.S. Supreme Court Justice	Sandra O'Connor 1981
First woman vice-presidential candidate	Geraldine Ferraro 1984
First American woman astronaut	Sally Ride 1983
First woman Formula 1 race driver	Lella Lombardi 1974
First widely syndicated cartoon-strip by a woman artist ("Brenda Starr")	Dale Messik 1940
First Olympic athlete to score a perfect 10.00 in any event	Nadia Comaneci 1976
First person to receive seven perfect scores as a gymnast	Nadia Comaneci 1976
First woman to receive the Nobel Prize for physics	Marie Curie 1903
First person to win two Nobel Prizes with the Nobel Prize for chemistry	Marie Curie, 1911
First woman to climb Mt. Everest	Junko Tabei 1975
First woman to sail solo around the world	Naomi James 1978
First woman to conduct the Metropolitan Opera	Sarah Caldwell 1976
First woman state governor	Nellie Tayloe Ross 1924
First woman airplane designer	Lillian Todd 1906
First woman dentist (officially earned degree)	Lucy B. Hobbs 1866
First woman foreign correspondent (Chicago Daily News)	Helen Kirkpatrick 1939
First woman president of the United Nations General Assembly	Vijayalakshmi Pandit 1953
First woman to receive the Nobel Prize for Literature	Selma Lagerlof 1909
First woman pilot to fly solo across the Atlantic	Amelia Earhart 1928
First American woman to win three gold medals at the Olympics in track and field	Wilma Rudolph 1960
First computer programmer	Ada Augusta Lovelace 1815
First woman to orbit the earth	Valentina Tereshkova-Nikolayeva 1963
First woman to own a baseball team (New York Mets)	Joan Whitney Payson 1962
First woman to win major Pulitzer Prize in Journalism	Anne O'Hare McCormick 1937
First woman boxing referee	Carol Polis 1973

Stereotypes Persist

One of the most amazing things about women who first moved into non-traditional careers is that they did so without female role models, and in the face of widespread social disapproval. You are fortunate to have women as role models now, but the old stereotypes have not disappeared.

Trudy's Story

Trudy discovered this when she decided to be an engineer. It was more difficult to be accepted into a college program than she thought it should have been, considering her excellent grades. When classes began, she found she was the only woman in some of her classes. All of her instructors were men. During lab, it seemed as if everyone was watching her, waiting for her to make a mistake. There didn't seem to be any women engineers on TV or in the movies. There certainly weren't any in the fashion magazines she read for relaxation.

Trudy began to feel like some kind of freak, and wondered if she wouldn't be better off as a teacher. But when she re-examined her values and personal goals, she realized that engineering held more rewards for her. She decided to stick with engineering, and is now glad she did. She feels it was unfair that she had to prove herself to her co-workers, simply because she was a woman; since she's shown them that she can work just as hard and just as well as they can, she's earned their respect. She loves her job and the financial security it provides.

Money Counts

Louise's Story

Louise enjoyed working with numbers, and knew she wanted that to be part of her job. But she wasn't sure if she should take a two-year vocational course to become a bookkeeper, or a college program, which would allow her to become an accountant. Louise looked up both jobs in the Occupational Outlook Handbook at the library. She was surprised to learn that, as a bookkeeper, she could expect to start at about $12,000 a year. As an accountant, she could start at about $19,000. If she went on to obtain certification as a public accountant, her earnings would be even greater. Louise decided accounting was the field for her.

Often, women think about a skill they have or the amount of training they want or can afford, and then automatically choose a traditional "woman's job." It's considered "safer" to take a traditional job, but taking a small risk can increase earning power greatly. By thinking just a bit more, women might see that there are other jobs in the same field that require no more training — and that pay *much more.*

It has only recently been acknowledged that many women work because they need money. In the past many people thought that women should only work until they married. If they worked after marriage, it was assumed that their salaries went only for "extras" or "luxuries." By pretending that women didn't have to support themselves or their families, employers could justify paying them less than men. Although we now know that women work for the same reasons that men do, the pattern remains: Jobs which have traditionally been held by women continue to pay less than comparable jobs which are usually held by men. That's one reason why you should consider a "man's job": You are quite likely to earn more money in a non-traditional career. If you love to travel or fly, for example, you have probably considered becoming a flight attendant. In that job you could expect to start at a salary of about $13,000 a year, working up to an average of $23,000 a year. But have you thought of becoming a pilot? Commercial airline pilots make an average salary of $80,000 a year by the age of 50. Of course, it takes more training, more commitment, greater risk, and different skills to become a pilot, but how do you know you couldn't do it?

Let's consider a few more examples. A cosmetologist makes on the average about $250-$400 a week, while a plumber can earn up to $585 a week. A person working as a bank teller earns $11,000 a year; a mail carrier can expect to earn $25,000 a year. A typist averages $15,000 while a tool and die maker can make $23,000. A sales clerk will probably start at $3.35/hr working up to an average of $288 per week. Wholesale trade salesworkers can earn $450 per week.

Beginning to see the pattern? Figures on these and thousands of other occupations are available from the *Occupational Outlook Handbook*, a volume published by the U.S. Department of Labor, and available at your local library. It will tell you not only how much you can expect to be paid for various jobs, but what kind of training is required, and whether or not there is a demand for people in that field. Next time you're at the library, ask to see it. It can be extremely helpful in making career decisions.

Where the Women are, the Money Isn't

Like it or not (and who could like it?), there is a connection between the number of women in various professional careers, and the salaries for those careers. Although plain old sex discrimination plays a part in the difference between what men and women earn, so does the type of career most women *choose*. The following table shows the percentage of women in different fields.[10]

Careers	Percentage of Women
Secretary	99.1
Nurse	94.4
Bank teller	92.9
Cosmetologist	83.3
Librarian	84.6
Elementary teacher	82.4
Doctor	22.8
Lawyer	20.2
Architect	13.3
Engineer	5.9
Truck driver	1.5
Electrician	1.7

Now let's see what the average salaries are for each career.

Careers	Salaries
Secretary	$17,000
Nurse (RN)	$21,000
Bank teller	$11,000
Cosmetologist	$17,000
College librarian (with Master's Degree)	$26,000
Elementary teacher	$23,000
Physician	$108,000
Lawyer (private practice with experience)	$88,000
Architect	$29,000
Engineer	$41,000
Truck driver	$25,000
Electrician	$23,000

The Importance of Math

Hilary's Story

In grade school, Hilary was a whiz at math. So were many of the other girls. At times when many of the boys were squirming at their desks, wrinkling their foreheads, and trying to count on their toes, Hilary and the girls had already finished the assignment and had moved on to the extra credit questions and puzzles. Her parents hardly noticed when she brought home A's in math. It happened so often that they just took it for granted.

Then, sometime in junior high school, all that changed. Like her friends, Hilary seemed to lose interest in math. Her grades dropped, but she didn't really care. The boys, on the other hand, seemed to have finally caught on. They were taking all the math offered and doing well in it now.

What happened to cause this turnabout? Did the girls become dumb for some reason? Did the boys drain the girls' math ability and use it for their own, like some mad scientist in a bad horror movie? No, of course not. There isn't a logical explanation, but what happened to Hilary does happen frequently to young women. It has nothing to do with ability. If you had ability in grade school, you still have it. What you may have lost is the motivation to learn math. What you may have acquired is the notion that math is "unfeminine" or "for brains only." You may think "No one wants to date girls who take trigonometry." If you do, that's silly.

You need to take math. Three years of high school math will give you more career options than almost any other subject. A great array of clerical jobs in banking, insurance, business, and government need workers with math skills.

If you're planning to go to college, taking some math classes in high school is essential. A year of algebra and one of geometry are a bare minimum. If you have any interest in science or engineering, you ought to take trigonometry and calculus, too. Many colleges will not *admit* you without a solid math background. Most majors that prepare you for a specific high-paying career require math, although the amount and kind may differ. The math an engineer or a chemist needs is different from that an economics or business major needs. In each case the solid high school math foundation is the same. Whatever your major, one thing is certain. A knowledge of math helps you think analytically, which is an asset in any job. If you have no idea of the career you would like to eventually pursue, take math in high school to be safe. In this way you will not eliminate potential majors or careers for lack of a high school math background.

Below is a list of some of the more common college majors. The "yes" or "no" beside each one indicates whether or not some college math is required for a degree in that major.

Major	Math Required	Major	Math Required
Anthropology	— no	Engineering	— yes
Architecture	— yes	English	— no
Art History	— no	French	— no
Astronomy	— yes	History	— no
Biology	— yes	Journalism	— no
Business	— yes	Mathematics	— yes
Chemistry	— yes	Music	— no
Classics	— no	Pharmacology	— yes
Computer Science	— yes	Philosophy	— yes
Earth Science	— yes	Physics	— yes
Economics	— yes	Political Science	— no
Environmental Studies	— yes	Psychology	— yes
Education	— no	Sociology	— no

Looking back at the list, you'll see that most majors not requiring advanced math don't lead to specific careers. What, for example, can you do with a major in English? You could go on to graduate school. A few people with *specific career plans* can make good use of the "no" majors. Some people with such majors are lucky and find jobs that interest them; and some corporations *like* to hire graduates with liberal arts backgrounds and then train them in the company's methods. You will usually find, however, that college graduates who are unemployed or in low-paying jobs have degrees that did not prepare them for a specific job.

Did You Know?[11]

With math in her background a young woman graduating from high school can expect to earn $2,000-$4,000 more in her first entry level job. Math is often the key to the non-traditional jobs that pay more and offer more upward mobility.

It is a myth that people good at math can instantly come up with right answers or correct procedures.

The average yearly salary offered to a graduate with a 1983 Bachelor of Science Degree in Petroleum Engineering was $31,044; with a Bachelor of Arts Degree in Humanities, $16,560.

These high-paying jobs require some college math.

    Doctors
    Nurses
    Pharmacists
    All science-related jobs
    examples:
        Engineers
        Physicists
        Geologists
        Oceanographers
        Architects
        Accountants
        Computer Programmers

A study in 1974 found that without 3-1/2 years of high school mathematics, entering students at the University of California at Berkeley found 3/4 of the college majors closed to them.

Math is not a talent, but a series of skills to be learned.

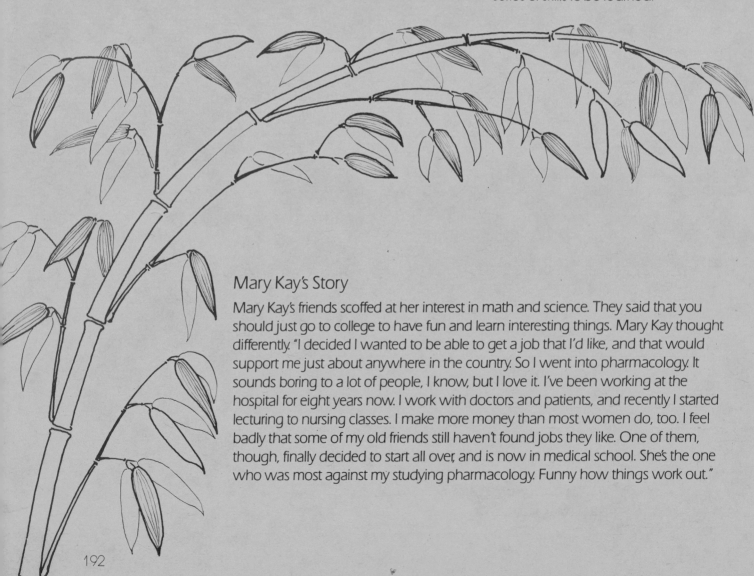

Mary Kay's Story

Mary Kay's friends scoffed at her interest in math and science. They said that you should just go to college to have fun and learn interesting things. Mary Kay thought differently. "I decided I wanted to be able to get a job that I'd like, and that would support me just about anywhere in the country. So I went into pharmacology. It sounds boring to a lot of people, I know, but I love it. I've been working at the hospital for eight years now. I work with doctors and patients, and recently I started lecturing to nursing classes. I make more money than most women do, too. I feel badly that some of my old friends still haven't found jobs they like. One of them, though, finally decided to start all over, and is now in medical school. She's the one who was most against my studying pharmacology. Funny how things work out."

Are You Giving Up a High-Paid Future for a Part-Time Job?

Jennifer's Story

Jennifer knew she should be taking geometry, but she just didn't know when she'd have time. She was working half-days at a boutique to save money for a car, and when she got home in the evening, she didn't seem to have enough energy for her homework. Giving up the job would mean losing not only her car, but the discount she received on clothes. She _did_ want to go to college, though. She wasn't sure what to do.

Is working part-time worth it to you? In some cases, there doesn't seem to be much choice. But if you don't have to work, is taking a job helping or hurting your future chances?

Ask five or more friends with jobs how much they are earning, and find the average. Chances are, it will be about $3.75 an hour. If so, and if your friends were working full time, their yearly salaries would be $7,800 ($3.75 per hour multiplied by 40 hours per week multiplied by 52 weeks per year). If working now means you can't take math classes in high school, maybe you should re-evaluate: Is it really worthwhile for you to work now?

Elective courses like math and science are usually the ones that get sacrificed to accommodate a schedule which includes a part-time job. If you are a capable student who doesn't have to work, you could be working yourself right out of a high-paying future for $3.75 an hour now. Should you do it? Ask yourself these questions.

1. Does my working part-time after school influence my decision on how difficult the courses I take are?

   _____

2. Does my working part-time after school affect the time I have available to do my homework and maintain my grades?

   _____

3. Does my after school job add to my job skills or train me for my chosen career field?

   _____

4. Do I need to work for economic reasons so that I can stay in school?

   _____

If you answered "yes" to question 1 or 2, or "no" to question 3 or 4, you need to re-evaluate your priorities.

REFLECTIONS

You must do the thing you think you
cannot do.
— Eleanor Roosevelt

If you can do it then why do it?
— Gertrude Stein

CHAPTER TEN

Putting It All Together

Career planning

There are many ways to approach career planning. You can ask your best friend what she's going to do, and do the same. You can ask your parents what they want you to do, and then do the opposite. You can put off making any plans in the hope that you'll never have to support yourself (after all, there are at least two bona fide, unmarried, English-speaking princes in the world). You can cling to your job fantasies, even if the obstacles are very evident. (Who *says* a jockey can't be 5'8'' and weigh 130 pounds?) Or, you can do it the right way.

As you've completed the exercises in this book, you have compiled a self-portrait. You know what kind of life style appeals to you, and how much it might cost to support yourself in that manner. You realize that you may well *have* to maintain it. You've thought about your values, your goals and your skills. You've considered the special delights and problems that come with having a family. Now you need to investigate some of the careers that appeal to you; careers that fit the person you are, the woman you hope to become.

Don't be inhibited about what you've done so far. This book is not "Your Life Plan," carved in stone. It's not something you'll be held to forever and ever. As you change, so may your plans. Change is a normal part of life. But don't change blindly. This chapter will teach you how to investigate the jobs that most appeal to you. The process will work just as well next year and the year after that. In fact, it can help you choose, throughout your life, the best job for a very unique person — you.

My Skills,
Aptitudes,
& Interests

_____
_____
_____
_____

My Family
Goals

_____
_____
_____

Who are You, Anyway?

Look over the information you've learned thus far. Fill in the balloons to get a picture of yourself.

Job Characteristics

My Values

_____

_____

_____

_____

My Goals

_____

_____

_____

_____

Now that you've reviewed a few of your own characteristics, let's look at some that are job-related. Four important considerations are listed below, along with some of the choices that go along with them. Choose one or two phrases from each category that best describe what you want in a job or work situation.

Environment

Outdoors
Pleasant indoor environment
Lovely office
Shop/garage/warehouse
Some outdoors/some indoors

Other _____
_____

Compensation

Security
High emotional rewards
Recognition in the community
Excitement/adventure
Weekly paycheck
High pay
Flexible time

Other _____
_____

Responsibility

Own boss
Low stress
Variety
Power
Freedom
Team work
Decision maker
Few decisions made
Support/assist/help

Other _____
_____

Working with:

People
Adults
Children
Senior Citizens
Poor
Animals
Machines
Hands
No one else

Other _____
_____

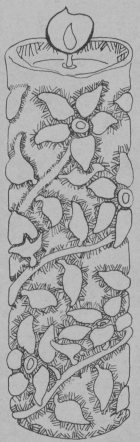

Everyone Can't be a Superstar

Considering all the things you know about yourself, what are two careers you think you might like? Be sure to consider all the alternatives. For example, it's easy to think of well-known glamour jobs, and jobs that have great appeal. You might think it would be fun to be a star like Brooke Shields. Unfortunately, those jobs are rare. However, if you look beyond the obvious, there are thousands and thousands of different jobs. For every superstar, there are dozens of people on the sidelines. The others may not get their pictures in the paper all the time, but they do take part in all the excitement, meet important people, travel and make a living at it. Perhaps you've never thought about all the "behind the scenes" jobs. Here are just a few of them, to get you started. Put on your thinking cap and see if you can come up with others and put them on the blank lines. Maybe one of them is *the* job for you.

Behind every television star there's a:

make-up artist	hairdresser	personal secretary
stunt person	photographer	answering service
wardrobe consultant	manager	accountant
agent	writer	caterer
_____	_____	_____
_____	_____	_____

Every brain surgeon needs a:

general physician	dietician	physical therapist
anesthetist	pharmacist	speech pathologist
hospital	secretary	occupational
administrator	x-ray technician	therapist
head nurse		counselor
_____	_____	_____
_____	_____	_____

A movie director can't operate without a:

camera operator	stage hand	props director
light technician	producer	publicity agent
set director	music director	electrician
film editor	cinematographer	special effects designer

_____   _____   _____

_____   _____   _____

Professional athletes use a:

coach	agent	statistician
equipment manager	sportscaster	photographer
doctor	referee/umpire	sportswriter
physical therapist	scoreboard operator	time keeper

_____   _____   _____

_____   _____   _____

If you can't be a rock musician, maybe you can be a:

disc jockey	sound editor	concert co-ordinator
recording technician	record producer	lighting director
piano tuner	song writer	costume desiger
album cover designer	cutting designer	dancer

_____   _____   _____

_____   _____   _____

The President of the United States has at least one:

advisor	chauffeur	Director of Protocol
assistant	pilot	White House tour guide
speech writer	chef	interior designer
security guard	secretary	press secretary

_____   _____   _____

_____   _____   _____

The Chief Executive Officer of a major oil corporation is backed by a:

corporate planner	lobbyist	computer programmer
accountant	geologist	data entry operator
lawyer	petroleum engineer	financial analyst
marketing manager	publicity director	researcher

_____   _____   _____

_____   _____   _____

What would you like to do? List two choices below. They might be in fields you've been thinking about for a long time, or they could be jobs that have occurred to you since you started doing these exercises. You don't have to know a lot about them. That's the purpose of this exercise. *Let your imagination soar here.*

1. _____

2. _____

Choose *one more* job from the following list. These are non-traditional careers that women often overlook even though they can be very rewarding and high-paying.

Carpenter	Plumber
Pilot	Architect
Telephone repairer	Garbage collector
Truck driver	Gardener
Computer programmer	Hotel manager
Doctor	Broadcaster
Auto mechanic	Insurance salesperson
Lawyer	City manager
Marine biologist	Accountant
Mechanical engineer	House painter
Police officer	Geologist
Stockbroker (account executive)	Welder

3. _____

Gathering Job Information

To find out about the jobs you've chosen, you'll need to go to your school or public library. *The Occupational Outlook Handbook* discussed in the previous chapter will give you much of the information you will need. Another good source is the *Dictionary of Occupational Titles*, or DOT. In addition, ask the librarian to direct you to the section with career materials. Here you'll find many books which may deal in greater depth with jobs you're investigating. For example, there may be recent books on jobs for women, blue collar jobs, technical jobs, sales, and so forth. Become familiar with these sources, because they can provide you with important facts and figures whenever you think of an interesting new job, or later in life, when you think you'd like to change careers.

Once you've selected the three careers you want to look at more closely, answer the following questions about each of them. Separate worksheets are included for each job.

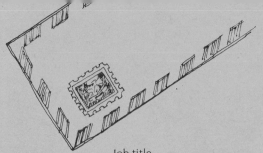

Job title _____

1. List specific activities to be performed on the job. (Some examples would be: "Carpenter — measuring, sawing, hammering, sanding; Lawyer — researching, writing, interviewing clients, giving speeches in courtroom.")

_____

_____

_____

_____

2. What is the job environment? Is the job done indoors or outdoors? In a large office? In a noisy factory?

_____

_____

3. What rewards does the job provide? High salary? Convenient hours? Emotional satisfaction? Pleasant surroundings? Adventure?

_____

_____

_____

4. Why would this job be particularly satisfying to *you*? Review your values, interests, and life goals for guidance here.

_____

_____

_____

5. How much training or education is required? Where could you get it? (Some examples are: a four-year degree from a university, six months at a business or trade school.) If possible, try to find a specific school or place where you could receive the training you would need. Not all colleges offer degrees in architecture, marine biology, and so forth.

_____

_____

_____

6. Are there any physical limitations? If so, what are they? (Strength requirements, health requirements, 20/20 vision, etc.)

_____

_____

_____

7. What is the approximate starting salary for this job? Mid-career salary?

_____

_____

_____

8. What is the projected outlook for this occupation? Will there be many jobs available when you are ready to enter the job market? Or are there few openings with much competition?

_____
_____
_____
_____

9. What aptitudes, strengths and talents are required?

_____
_____
_____
_____

10. How can you begin today to prepare for this career?

_____
_____
_____
_____

11. What classes do you need to take in high school to pursue this career?

_____
_____
_____

12. Where would you find employment in this job in your community or state?

_____
_____
_____
_____

Job title _____

1. List specific activities to be performed on the job. (Some examples would be: "Carpenter — measuring, sawing, hammering, sanding; Lawyer — researching, writing, interviewing clients, giving speeches in courtroom.")

_____
_____
_____
_____

2. What is the job environment? Is the job done indoors or outdoors? In a large office? In a noisy factory?

_____
_____

3. What rewards does the job provide? High salary? Convenient hours? Emotional satisfaction? Pleasant surroundings? Adventure?

_____

_____

_____

4. Why would this job be particularly satisfying to *you*? Review your values, interests, and life goals for guidance here.

_____

_____

_____

_____

5. How much training or education is required? Where could you get it? (Some examples are: a four-year degree from a university, six months at a business or trade school.) If possible, try to find a specific school or place where you could receive the training you would need. Not all colleges offer degrees in architecture, marine biology, and so forth.

_____

_____

_____

_____

6. Are there any physical limitations? If so, what are they? (Strength requirements, health requirements, 20/20 vision, etc.)

_____

_____

_____

7. What is the approximate starting salary for this job? Mid-career salary?

_____

_____

_____

8. What is the projected outlook for this occupation? Will there be many jobs available when you are ready to enter the job market? Or are there few openings with much competition?

_____

_____

_____

9. What aptitudes, strengths and talents are required?

_____

_____

_____

10. How can you begin today to prepare for this career?

_____

_____

_____

11. What classes do you need to take in high school to pursue this career?

_____

_____

_____

12. Where would you find employment in this job in your community or state?

_____

_____

_____

Job title _____

1. List specific activities to be performed on the job. (Some examples would be: "Carpenter — measuring, sawing, hammering, sanding; Lawyer — researching, writing, interviewing clients, giving speeches in courtroom.")

_____

_____

_____

_____

2. What is the job environment? Is the job done indoors or outdoors? In a large office? In a noisy factory?

_____

_____

3. What rewards does the job provide? High salary? Convenient hours? Emotional satisfaction? Pleasant surroundings? Adventure?

_____

_____

_____

4. Why would this job be particularly satisfying to *you*? Review your values, interests, and life goals for guidance here.

_____

_____

_____

_____

5. How much training or education is required? Where could you get it? (Some examples are: a four-year degree from a university, six months at a business or trade school.) If possible, try to find a specific school or place where you could receive the training you would need. Not all colleges offer degrees in architecture, marine biology, and so forth.

_____

_____

_____

_____

6. Are there any physical limitations? If so, what are they? (Strength requirements, health requirements, 20/20 vision, etc.)

_____

_____

_____

7. What is the approximate starting salary for this job? Mid-career salary?

_____

_____

_____

8. What is the projected outlook for this occupation? Will there be many jobs available when you are ready to enter the job market? Or are there few openings with much competition?

_____

_____

_____

_____

9. What aptitudes, strengths and talents are required?

_____

_____

_____

_____

10. How can you begin today to prepare for this career?

_____

_____

_____

_____

11. What classes do you need to take in high school to pursue this career?

_____

_____

_____

12. Where would you find employment in this job in your community or state?

_____

_____

_____

Ask an Expert

Another valuable way to learn *a lot* about careers is to interview someone who already does the work you're considering. Just calling someone you may not even know, and asking her or him to spend some time with you, may sound frightening, but don't worry. This technique, called the informational interview, is highly recommended by many employment counselors and career experts. Most people love to talk about themselves, and will be happy to give you an appointment. Just remember that this person is probably making room for you in a tight schedule, so be on time, be polite, and don't stay longer than you said you would. Afterwards, send a thank-you note. Use this technique to interview someone currently working in each of the occupations that interests you.

If you don't know the name of someone working in the field you wish to investigate, ask your friends, parents or teachers. Consult a phone book, a librarian, the Chamber of Commerce, professional organizations, unions, an agricultural extension agent, an employment office, or another source which might deal with people in that profession.

Once you have a name and phone number, you're set to make a call. You might start the conversation by saying something like this: "Hello, Ms. Jones. This is Susie Smith. I'm interested in becoming a doctor and my teacher, Betty Johnson, suggested I talk with you to get a better idea of what it's like. Would you be able to spare half an hour to answer some of my questions?"

The questionnaire provided here will help you guide the interview.

INTERVIEW QUESTIONNAIRE

Job title _____

Male or female? (You shouldn't need to ask this one!) _____

How many years have you been in this job? _____
_____

What is your personal educational history? _____
_____
_____
_____

If you had your educational years to live over again, what would you do differently?
_____
_____

What advice would you give me as I begin my career search and preparation?
_____
_____

What do you like best about your job?
_____
_____

What do you like least about your job?
_____
_____

Do you foresee a career change before you retire?
_____
_____

If so, to what type of work? _____
_____
_____

Getting Experience

Once you think you've made a decision and know which career you want to pursue, there's a valuable step you can take. It will either reinforce your decision, or help you change your mind before you've invested a great deal of time and money. It's this: Get experience in your chosen field. Of course, a high school student can't go out and get a job as a surgeon or an architect. However, you can usually find something to do that will put you in contact with the job and the people who do it. You may have to take a part-time or summer job at the minimum wage to run errands in an engineering office or at a construction site, or wherever your prospective job is performed. Would you like to be a chef? A waitressing job or one as a preparations assistant in the kitchen would help you decide. What would it be like to be a trial lawyer? Attend a court trial to learn. What does an urban planner do? You could see one in action by attending a city planning commission meeting. Interested in communications? Visit a TV or radio station and find out what the people you see and hear do when they're not in front of a camera or microphone. Even if you have to *volunteer* your time, you'll find it worthwhile.

Pat's Story

Pat, for example, wanted to be a lawyer. She passed up a higher-paying job flipping hamburgers to run errands at a local law firm. She learned what goes on in a law firm. That made her more determined than ever to go through with her law school plans. Just being in the environment also helped her pick up a lot of information which made her school work easier. She could see why different classes were important, and was less tempted to let her work slip. All this time the lawyers in the office encouraged her and observed her progress. When she graduated from law school, they offered her a job. Today she is a partner in the firm.

Mindy's Story

Mindy, on the other hand, had been sure since the second grade that she wanted to be a veterinarian. She loved animals, and the course work was easy enough. The summer after her junior year of college, she took a job at a veterinary clinic. She hated it. She didn't like the hours. She realized that this would stand in the way of a family life. She found the tasks boring and repetitive, because only a small percentage of the time was spent in surgery. Though it was difficult for her to give up her dream, she decided that she needed a more creative job with more freedom and more varied duties. Fortunately, she changed her plans before spending four years in veterinary school. Of course, she didn't give up her passion for animals—she now breeds thoroughbred horses as a sideline.

What about you? How can you get first-hand experience in your chosen career? Whatever you have to do, or whatever else you have to give up, it will be one of the most valuable experiences you can have!

Your Goals

By now you should have some ideas about what you want for your future, in terms of both your career and your family. What are your goals for high school and beyond?

HIGH SCHOOL YEARS

Goal _____

Objectives _____

_____

_____

Goal _____

Objectives _____

_____

_____

AFTER HIGH SCHOOL, COLLEGE, OR TRADE SCHOOL

Goal _____

Objectives _____

_____

_____

Goal _____

Objectives _____

_____

_____

REFLECTIONS

If there's a will, there's a way.

CHAPTER ELEVEN

Yes, You Can!

Financial aid for school or training

Where do you go from here? Chances are, you'll need some type of training after high school. That might mean college, junior college, vocational or business school or an apprenticeship. Whatever you choose, it will probably require money, and that's why a lot of people get discouraged. Don't let yourself be one of them.

Financial aid is available to almost everyone — *if* you know where to look, and, if you keep these two rules in mind:

1. Apply for every type of aid for which you are qualified.
2. Apply on time.

The beginning of your junior year is not too soon to start your search for financial aid. Certainly you should begin by the summer before your senior year. Where should you look? Information is readily available. Look in libraries, book stores, and career centers, under the topic of "financial aid" or "student financial aid." Your school counselor receives all the latest bulletins, and should have files of local aid sources. The schools you are applying to also have extensive, free financial aid information. You need only write to the school and request it.

What school should you contact? At this point, you probably don't know where you want to go, much less where you'll be accepted. Get all the information you can to assure that you make the best choice. Write for bulletins and financial aid information from many sources: private colleges, state universities, state colleges, junior colleges and vocational-technical schools.

Before choosing schools, you will need to know approximately how much money you will need for the following items.

*   Tuition and fees (stated in school catalogue)
*   Books and supplies (approximations stated in the catalogue)
*   Room and board (The cost for living on campus is stated in the catalogue. Otherwise, use cost of living at home or in an apartment.)
*   Transportation (daily, if commuting from home; two round trips per year, if school is distant)
*   Personal expenses (clothing, laundry, recreation, etc.)

Compare sample budgets for each of the schools you are considering.

ESTIMATED EXPENSES

	Sample Budget	First College Choice	Second College Choice	Third College Choice
Tuition	$3,000	_____	_____	_____
Books and supplies	300	_____	_____	_____
Room and board	1,700	_____	_____	_____
Personal items	600	_____	_____	_____
Transportation	400	_____	_____	_____
Other	_____	_____	_____	_____
TOTAL	$6,000	_____	_____	_____

ESTIMATED RESOURCES

	Sample Budget	First College Choice	Second College Choice	Third College Choice
Less Parents' contribution	$1,000	_____	_____	_____
Summer savings	500	_____	_____	_____
Student savings	300	_____	_____	_____
Other	_____	_____	_____	_____
TOTAL	$1,800	_____	_____	_____
Equals ADDITIONAL FUNDS NEEDED	$4,200	_____	_____	_____

For most types of aid, you and your family are expected to contribute as much as you are able. This amount is determined by completing an application which takes into account the size and income of your family. By subtracting the expected family contribution from the total estimate for your year's expenses, you will come up with the amount of financial aid you need. Until the standardized needs assessment is completed, you will not know exactly what you or your family are expected to contribute. Do not wait to find this figure before applying. It will be too late. Remember that you are under no obligation to accept anything until you formally enroll in the school. Then you can determine if the package and the program meet your needs.

To maximize your chances for a favorable package, you should normally apply for financial aid at the same time you apply for enrollment. It is highly recommended that you contact the financial aid officer at your chosen school nine months to a year before you plan to enroll.

Ninety percent of all financial aid is channeled through financial aid officers at post high school educational facilities. We repeat: You should learn what's available, and apply to the appropriate sources on time. It will, literally, pay off.

What is Available?

Financial aid is of three types:

- Gift aid
- Loans
- Work study

GIFT AID: SCHOLARSHIPS AND GRANTS

Scholarships and grants are paid to the student or the school and do not have to be repaid. Sometimes they are based on financial need, but in other cases, they are awarded on the basis of academic achievement or some other specific criteria, such as participation in athletics, excellence in music, art, or writing. There are also a large number of restricted grants or scholarships. Qualifying for these depends on having a particular ethnic background, or religious affiliation, or on being the child of a company employee.

Be sure to search widely. There are literally thousands of grants and scholarships available.

LOANS

Loans, unlike gift aid, must be paid back, usually with interest. The interest rate is usually much lower than the commercial interest rate, and the terms allow recipients to pay back their loans after they finish school.

WORK-STUDY

Additional sources of financing can be obtained from student employment or work-study programs. Often the jobs available are related to your chosen field of study and can provide valuable experience. Work-study jobs are also flexible enough to meet the time commitments of students.

In addition, you may be eligible for other specific benefits. Support from railroad or veteran's benefits, are available to many families. The military also offers its own plans for education and training.

ANOTHER OPTION: WORKING YOUR WAY THROUGH

You might consider the possibility of working your way through college or trade school. It's not easy, and it may take you a little longer to graduate, but it can be done in a number of ways.

If you can live at home, or if you have saved some money, you may be able to make ends meet just by working part-time during the school year and full-time over the summer. If you need a full-time income, you may have to take fewer classes each term. In many schools, degrees in some subjects can be earned entirely through evening classes. Or, you might want to work full-time, save your money, and postpone your education for a year or two.

If your efforts don't initially produce a source of financial aid, keep looking. You've come too far to turn back now.

The adventure's just beginning.

REFLECTIONS

We should all be concerned about
the future because we will have to
spend the rest of our lives there.
— Charles F. Kettering

CHAPTER TWELVE

What Are You Doing For the Rest of Your Life?

Exercises for the future

Time is a dressmaker specializing in
alterations.
— Faith Baldwin

Way back in the beginning of this book, we promised that this would be your story. If we've been at all successful, you realize by now that what happens to you from here onward is pretty much up to you. You are the author of your own life story.

In these pages, you can record the changes that will take place as you get older. You can expect substantial changes in your goals and values. And, whatever your age, there will always be new decisions to be made. The skills you have acquired while working through this journal will prove useful throughout your life. When your world seems particularly puzzling, you may want to refer back to the appropriate chapter and review how to make a decision, or how to figure out what it is that you want.

Use the following pages to help you remember where you've been, and where you're heading. Someday you might want to pass your book on to a granddaughter or other young woman. We hope that the messages you'll give to her will be full of hope, fulfillment, and resounding success!

In My Twenties

Photo

Date: _____

Thoughts about relationships:

Experiences I've found most valuable or satisfying:

What I value now:

My family plans and goals:

Important decisions I must make:

How I spend my time:

New skills and interests:

My goals for the next ten years:

In My Thirties

Photo

Date _____

Values I'd like to instill in my children:

Experiences I've found most valuable or satisfying:

What I value now:

My family plans and goals:

Important decisions I must make:

How I spend my time:

New skills and interests:

My goals for the next ten years:

In My Forties

Photo

Date _____

Mid-life changes I'm considering:

Experiences I've found most valuable or satisfying:

What I value now:

My family plans and goals:

Important decisions I must make:

How I spend my time:

New skills and interests:

My goals for the next ten years:

In My Fifties

Photo

Date _____

How I feel about getting older:

Experiences I've found most valuable or satisfying:

What I value now:

My family plans and goals:

Important decisions I must make:

How I spend my time:

New skills and interests:

My goals for the next ten years:

My Sixties and Beyond

Photo

Date _____

How I feel about retirement:

Experiences I've found most valuable or satisfying:

What I value now:

My family plans and goals:

Important decisions I must make:

How I spend my time:

New skills and interests:

My goals for the next ten years:

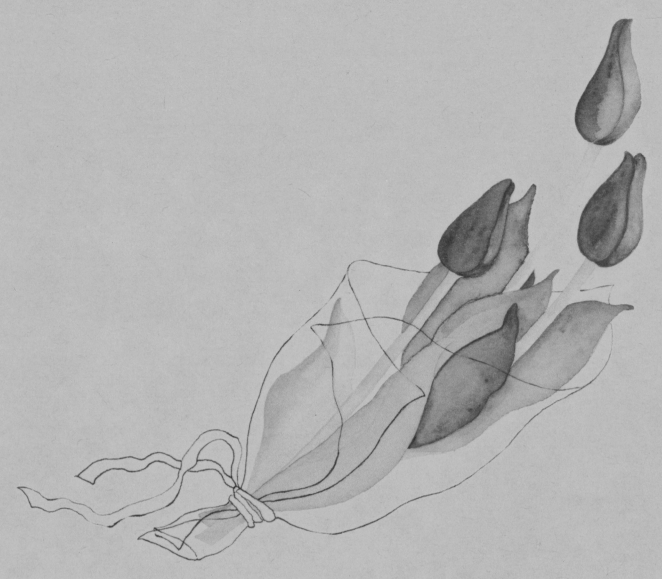

Some Special Situations

In living your life, you will encounter some special situations. These are the "biggies," the turning points in your life and the decisions that can have a lasting effect on you and on others. You won't come across all of the situations, but some are sure to occur.

The exercises that follow will be helpful when you find yourself confused, lost, or just overwhelmed. Look through them briefly now, and make a mental note that they're here to help you when, and if, the time comes.

Should I Marry This Man?

Having always considered yourself a fairly normal person, you've lately taken to washing your hair with toothpaste, trying to put your underwear on over your head, and calling your little brother "Love Bunny." In short, you're in love. It's a wonderful time, a wonderful feeling, but is it the "real thing"? Should you marry this man?

This is one of the most important decisions you will ever make. What's best for you? The following exercise will help you decide.

The first question to ask yourself is, "Is this the right time for me to get married?" Also, ask yourself, "Am I both emotionally and financially ready for this commitment?"

Use the decision-making process discussed earlier, on page 133, to work through this question.

1. Your goal: _____

_____

Alternative	Advantages	Disadvantages	Probable Outcome

What About Your Values?

Husbands and wives who share similar values are more likely to have successful marriages. Do you and your fiancé share the same values? Have you re-examined *your* values recently? If not, this is the time to do it. Go back to pages 93-97 for review. Then, when you've completed this exercise, ask your fiancé to fill it out too. Compare your answers.

Your values   Date _____   Your fiancé's values   Date _____

_____   _____

_____   _____

_____   _____

What are your values concerning children?

	You	Your Fiancé
To have?	_____	_____
When?	_____	_____
How many?	_____	_____
Childcare?	_____	_____

Marrying someone whose goals coincide with yours also increases your chance for happiness. Review the section on goal setting starting on page 106. Then, sit down with your fiancé and write some goals and objectives as they relate to:

Your Relationship

Goal _____

Objectives _____

_____

Family/Children

Goal _____

Objectives _____

_____

Career/Work/Economics

Goal _____

Objectives _____

_____

Your Environment/Locale/Housing

Goal _____

Objectives _____

_____

Now That I'm a Mother

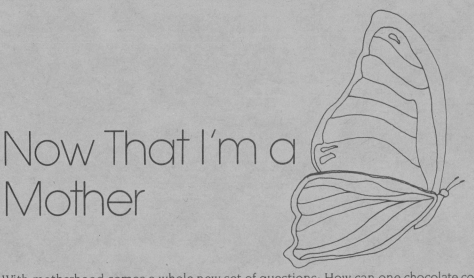

With motherhood comes a whole new set of questions: How can one chocolate cookie stretch far enough to cover three chairs, two walls, and an entire two-year-old child? If your maternity ward roommate left the hospital in a pair of size 8 jeans, why are you, six months later, still in maternity pants? Is there a physiological reason why men do not hear the cries of their children during Monday night football or anytime between the hours of midnight and seven a.m.? With all these weighty matters on your mind, you probably haven't had time to think about the kinds of values you hope to instill in your child.

But it's a fact that many values are formed during the pre-school and early school years. Review the values section of this book, pages 87 to 102. From the list provided there, choose the ones you think you would like your children to grow up with. List them here.

_____

_____

_____

_____

Now think of ways you can expose your children to an appreciation for these values, starting now. Write some goals and objectives below. For example, if your goal is to raise independent children, your objectives might include making sure that they are responsible for certain household chores, or restraining yourself from doing things for your children that they are capable of doing for themselves.

Goal _____

Objectives _____

_____

Goal _____

Objectives _____

_____

Goal _____

Objectives _____

_____

Messages I'd Like to Give My Daughter

Back on page 18, you completed an exercise which asked you to consider what messages you would give your daughter on the importance of success in school, appearance, marriage, career, and children. Now that you actually do have a daughter, review that exercise. Have your ideas changed? The passage of time and the realities of adult life make it highly likely. We've reprinted the entire exercise here to let you either re-affirm or re-evaluate your plan. Only this time, we're asking you to think about ways in which you can deliver the messages, as well. Write your messages and action plans below.

Success in School: _____

    Action Plan: _____

Appearance: _____

    Action Plan: _____

Marriage: _____

    Action Plan: _____

Career: _____

    Action Plan: _____

Children: _____

    Action Plan: _____

Let's not leave out the boys. If we hope to achieve an improved life for women, we'll need the help of the other half of humanity. What messages would you like to give your son, and how might you get those messages across to him? Complete the exercise again with your male child in mind.

Success in School: _____

    Action Plan: _____

Appearance: _____

    Action Plan: _____

Marriage: _____

    Action Plan: _____

Career: _____

    Action Plan: _____

Children: _____

    Action Plan: _____

Help for the Overwhelmed

Looking back, when you were young and someone asked you what you were going to be when you grew up, would the most truthful answer have been "tired"? If so, this exercise may help you get a grip on things. Use it when it all gets to be too much — when you're trying to balance family responsibilities, a career, a relationship, civic activities, possibly a family crisis, and you just can't seem to say "no" to even the most unreasonable requests.

Review the material concerning time management on pages 168-171. Then, in the space provided here, list all the tasks you have to do in the next week. Place an A, B, or C next to each to indicate its importance. Next to each C, write an assertive response to use when informing someone of your inability to complete the task.

Continue this practice each week until you gain better control of your time and well-being.

_____ _____

_____ _____

_____ _____

_____ _____

_____ _____

_____ _____

_____ _____

_____ _____

An Exercise for Everyone

PLANNING FOR THE UNFORESEEN

No matter how well you've planned, or how well things seem to be going, circumstances can change drastically overnight. Review the stories on pages 49 to 54 for a small sample of what can go wrong. If you suddenly found you needed to support yourself, could you do it? It's dangerous not to have an alternate plan. Therefore, everyone should do this economic inventory to see where she stands. The twelfth anniversary of owning this book might be a good time to check out your capacity for survival.

My income per month, or what I could reasonably expect to earn if I got a job tomorrow: $_____.

Monthly expenses today:

Housing	$ _____
Transportation	$ _____
Clothing	$ _____
Food	$ _____
Entertainment	$ _____
Furnishings	$ _____
Health care	$ _____
Child care	$ _____
Savings	$ _____
Miscellaneous	$ _____
TOTAL	$ _____

If your monthly budget totals more than you now make, or could expect to earn, revise the figures until you've arrived at a budget you could meet.

Housing	$ _____
Transportation	$ _____
Clothing	$ _____
Food	$ _____
Entertainment	$ _____
Furnishings	$ _____
Health care	$ _____
Child care	$ _____
Savings	$ _____
Miscellaneous	$ _____
TOTAL	$ _____

Notes on what you had to eliminate from your budget:

_____

_____

_____

How do you feel about your situation? Think of an action plan which would let you feel more comfortable, and state it here:

Goal _____

Objectives _____

_____

_____

Should I Change Careers?

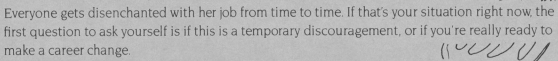

Everyone gets disenchanted with her job from time to time. If that's your situation right now, the first question to ask yourself is if this is a temporary discouragement, or if you're really ready to make a career change.

There is naturally some risk involved in changing jobs. But, there may be a risk in staying where you are, as well. (If, for example, the job doesn't pay enough for you to live on, if you're nearing the point of career burnout, or, if you know that your company is in danger of going out of business) Review the ideas on pages 137-139 to help evaluate and deal with the risks in your particular situation. Dissatisfaction with your present career may be the result of a change in values. What were your values when you took your present job?

_____

_____

What are they now?

_____

_____

Are there external forces prompting this change? (For example, a need for more money, a need for more time, or a desire to relocate)

_____

_____

Are the risks involved in making a change worth taking? Use the process outlined on page 139 to help you make your decision.

Goal: _____

Alternative	Advantages	Disadvantages	Probable Outcome

If you made a decision, think of an action plan to help you reach your goal.

Goal: _____

Objectives: _____

_____

I've Decided to Change Careers

You've decided to make a career change. Whether you're seeking a job that offers more pay, more potential, more commitment, less time, or less frustration, this career research exercise will help you choose wisely and put your plan into action. Ask yourself the following questions about your new direction and the career you think you want.

Job title _____

1. List specific activities to be performed on the job.

_____
_____
_____

2. What is the job environment? Is the job done indoors or outdoors? In a large office? In a noisy factory?

_____
_____
_____

3. What rewards does the job provide? High salary? Convenient hours? Emotional satisfaction? Pleasant surroundings? Adventure?

_____
_____
_____

4. Why would this job be particularly satisfying to *you*? Review your values, interests, and life goals for guidance here.

_____
_____
_____

5. How much training or education is required? Where could you get it?

_____
_____
_____

6. Are there any physical limitations? If so, what are they? (Strength requirements, health requirements, 20/20 vision, etc.)

_____
_____
_____

7. What is the approximate starting salary for this job? Mid-career salary?

_____

_____

_____

8. What is the projected outlook for this occupation? Are there many jobs available, or are there few openings and much competition?

_____

_____

_____

9. What aptitudes, strengths or talents are required?

_____

_____

_____

10. How can you begin today to prepare for this career?

_____

_____

_____

11. What classes do you need to take to pursue this career?

_____

_____

_____

12. Where would you find employment in this job in your locale?

_____

_____

_____

13. How will this change affect your family?

_____

_____

_____

Filling the Gaps

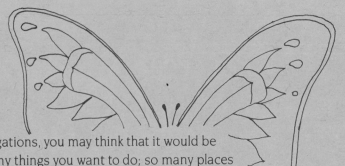

When your life is running over with family and career obligations, you may think that it would be paradise to have all that time to yourself. There are so many things you want to do; so many places you want to go. Then, when you find yourself with time on your hands — whether because the children have left home, you are widowed or divorced, or you've reached that longed-for retirement — you don't know what to do with it. Your dreams of the past may seem silly or extravagant, or maybe you've bought into the myth that you're too old to try anything new. Of course, you're not! You've earned this time, so go ahead and make it the rewarding part of your life it's meant to be! The exercise below will help you recapture some of those old dreams, and put you on your way to making them come true.

My hobbies and avocations are:

_____

_____

_____

I keep current and active in these areas by:

_____

_____

_____

If I had three wishes, they would be:

1. _____

2. _____

3. _____

What I can do, starting now, to make sure my wishes become a reality.

Goal _____

Objectives _____

_____

Goal _____

Objectives _____

_____

Goal _____

Objectives _____

_____

My Retirement

Retirement can be a shock to your system. You're used to being active; your days have been structured with work you valued and were rewarded for. It's not uncommon for a retired person to feel bored, restless, and unneeded. But it's wholly unnecessary to feel that way. You still have the wisdom and the talents you've developed over the years. You only need to find some new outlets for them.

Turn back to the skills identification exercise on page 178. Think of all the skills you've added since then, and write them here.

What an impressive list! Don't let your talents be lost to the world. Think of all the ways you can put this tremendous reservoir of skills to use. Maybe you'd like to start a part-time business or do volunteer work for a social service agency. There are hundreds of possibilities. Write down all you can think of here, and put the vitality back into your life!

My Legacy to the World

You've touched thousands of lives during your years on this earth. You've had friends and enemies, successes and failures, satisfaction and regret. Though much will be forgotten, your life will have an impact on those around you. Have you considered what kind of impact you would like that to be?

I would like to be remembered for:

An open letter to my granddaughters, grandnieces, their daughters, and the generations that follow me.

Date _____

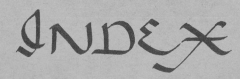

INDEX

NOTES

1. Twilla C. Liggett, Patricia L. R. Stevens, and Nan S. Schmeling, *The Whole Person Book: Toward Self-Discovery & Life Options*, under a grant from the Women's Educational Equity Act Program, U.S. Department of Education (Newton, MA: Education Development Center, 1979), pp. 175-176.

2. Coon, Dennis. *Introduction to Psychology: Exploration and Application*, 2d ed. (St. Paul, MN: West Publishing Co., 1980).

3. Inge K. Broverman, Donald M. Broverman, Frank E. Clarkson, Paul S. Rosenkrantz, and Susan R. Vogel, "Sex Role Stereotypes and Clinical Judgements of Mental Health," *Journal of Consulting and Clinical Psychology*: (1970), vol. 34, no. 1, pp. 1-7. Copyright by the American Psychological Association. Adapted by permission of the publisher and authors.

   Also adapted from Liggett, Stevens and Schmeling, *The Whole Person Book: Toward Self-Discovery & Life Options*.

4. See *20 Facts on Women Workers*, U.S. Department of Labor, Office of the Secretary, Women's Bureau (1986) for quiz nos. 2, 4, 5, 7, 10; no. 6 (1980).

   See *Today's Girls — Tomorrow's Women*, (A National Seminar, June 13-15, 1978, Wingspread Conference Center, Racine, Wisconsin, reprint ed., Girls Clubs of America, Inc., 1980) for quiz nos. 1, 9.

   See Liggett, Stevens and Schmeling, *The Whole Person Book: Toward Self-Discovery & Life Options*, for quiz no. 8.

   Current Population Survey, March 1985 Supplement — Bureau of Labor Statistics Department of Labor, for quiz no. 3.

5. Richard Boyer and David Savageau, *Places Rated Almanac: Your Guide to Finding the Best Places to Live in America* (Rand McNally and Co., 1985).

6. U.S. Department of Agriculture, Human Nutrition Information Service, Consumer Nutrition Center (Hyattsville, Md.).

7. H. B. Gelatt, Barbara Varenhorst, and Richard Carey, *Deciding* (New Jersey: College Board Publications, 1972), p 12.

8. Ibid., p. 44.

9. We learned about the Egg Baby Exercise from Charlotte Williams, San Marcos High School, Santa Barbara, Calif.

10. Earl F. Mellor, "Weekly Earnings in 1983: A Look at More Than 200 Occupations", *Monthly Labor Review*, January 1985, "Research Summaries".

11. Sheila Tobias, "Girls and Mathematics: Overcoming Anxiety and Avoidance," *Voice for Girls* (New York: Girls Clubs of America, Inc., Fall 1982), vol. 26, no. 3.

    Manpower Comments. Washington D.C. Scientific Manpower Commission, Vol. 20, No. 4, May 1983.

    Manpower Comments. Vol. 20, No. 7, September 1983.

ILLUSTRATIONS

Rose Margaret Braiden — Cover, pages 1, 2, 3, 4, 5, 6-7, 8-9, 10-11, 34-35, 44-45, 86-87, 114-115, 140-141, 150-151, 172-173, 180-181, 194-195, 210-211, 216-217

Pam Hoeft — pages 56, 57, 58, 64-65, 66, 69, 70, 72, 73, 74, 75, 77, 80, 90-91, 104, 112, 113, 148, 209.

Itoko Maeno — pages 12, 13, 16, 17, 18, 19, 20, 21, 22, 24, 25, 26, 27, 28, 29, 30, 31, 32, 33, 36, 37, 39, 40-41, 42, 46, 49, 50, 51, 52, 53, 54, 55, 59, 60-61, 62-63, 78-79, 82, 83, 84, 85, 88, 89, 92, 94, 95, 96, 97, 98, 99, 100, 101, 102, 103, 105, 106, 107, 108, 110, 116, 117, 118, 119, 120-121, 122, 123, 124, 128, 130, 131, 132, 134, 135, 136, 137, 138, 142, 144, 146, 147, 149, 152, 153, 154-155, 156, 157, 158, 160-161, 162, 163, 164, 166, 167, 168, 170-171, 174, 175, 177, 179, 182, 185, 186, 187, 188, 189, 190, 192, 193, 196-197, 198, 200, 201, 202, 204, 206, 208, 212, 214-215, 218, 219, 220, 221, 222, 223, 224, 227, 229, 231, 232-233, 235, 237, 238.

ACKNOWLEDGMENTS

Writing this book has been a wonderful adventure. We are grateful to the many caring and talented individuals who helped us along the way.

The Alice Tweed Tuohy Foundation funded the original project "Future Planning for Young Women" from which this book was developed. A grant from the James Irvine Foundation enabled us to produce and print such a beautiful workbook. The confidence and support of both these foundations is truly appreciated.

First Commodity Corporation of Boston, the Security Pacific Bank of Los Angeles, and the Atlantic Richfield Foundation generously contributed additional financial support, for which we sincerely thank them.

We are energized by the interest and support of Girls Clubs of America, Inc., particularly by Edith B. Phelps, former Executive Director; Martha Bernstein, Jane Quinn, Heather Johnston Nicholson, Jid Sprague, Marty Newsom, Mary Jo Gallo, and Margaret Gates, the present Executive Director.

We are very grateful to the Board of Directors of the Girls Club of Santa Barbara, especially Jean Goodrich, Perri Harcourt, and Bill Sheehan. Without the board's unflagging support and interest, the road to publication would have been long and hard.

Much of the credit for the successful completion of this book goes to the combined efforts of a large number of people in our community. The Santa Barbara Scholarship Foundation and Planned Parenthood of Santa Barbara provided excellent curriculum material. Bill Jackson, co-principal of Santa Barbara High School, and his staff gave us our original start by allowing us to use and test this book at Santa Barbara High School. Raymond Hill at Carpinteria High School and Doyle Tunnell of Laguna Blanca School also enthusiastically supported this project. We appreciated the suggestions and criticisms of students at these schools, especially Carol Cleek, Lois Estrada, Kendra Heidleberger, Cheryl Karpeles, Kara Moore, Paula Neary, Angelique Rix, Kimberly Sweeney, and Leslie Yenni.

For an abundance of inspiration, help and technical know-how, we thank Alma Allen, Jean Feigenbaum, Harriet Feinstein, Annie Fowler, Nancy Franco, Jim Godfrey, Fiona Hill, Lorraine Hoelscher, Michelle Jackman, Marsha Morrell, Hope Nexsen, Penelope Paine, Dr. Bert Pearlman, Diane Powers, Dan Poynter of Para Press, Jan Roberta, Linda Schwartz, Helen Shorrock, Josephine W. Van Schaick, Theo Thomas, Gloria Weston, Charlotte Williams, and Dia Zimmermann, typesetter.

Bouquets are due Margaret Dodd for the production and lovely design of this book, Rose Margaret Braiden, Pam Hoeft, and Itoko Maeno for the beautiful art work, and Friedrich Typography and Jostens for their fine technical efforts. Their combined talents have brought our words to life.

We are indebted to Cynthia Sweeney for her long hours of data entry and her patience and good humor during manuscript preparation.

Special thanks go to Dennis Coon for taking time from the revision of his text to edit this book. His extensive suggestions and re-writing have made this a much better book.

Barbara Greene and Sevren Coon worked many evenings and weekends copy editing and attending to hundreds of other details that were a part of producing this book. We thank them for their untiring devotion to this project.

Mindy Bingham, Judy Edmonson, Sandy Stryker